Dr. Eric J. Dingwall. Courtesy Mary Evans Picture Library, London.

TO THE MEMORY OF THE LATE ERIC J. DINGWALL, WHOSE RELENTLESS SEARCH FOR THE TRUTH ABOUT DANIEL DUNGLAS HOME LED HIM VERY CLOSE TO THE SOLUTION, AND MADE IT MUCH EASIER FOR THOSE WHO HAVE FOLLOWED HIM.

I am on "nobody's side" except when I am of the opinion, right or wrong, that a particular side is in the right in some particular controversy.

—Eric J. Dingwall in a letter to R. George Medhurst on 27 March 1964

Glendower: "I can call spirits from the vasty deep."
Hotspur: "Why, so can I, or so can any man;
But will they come when you do call for them?"

Shakespeare's *Henry IV, Part I*, Act 3, Scene 1, 51–53

The SORCERER of KINGS

Gordon Stein, Ph.D.
Foreword by James Randi

The Case of Daniel Dunglas Home and William Crookes

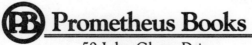 **Prometheus Books**
59 John Glenn Drive
Buffalo, NewYork 14228-2197

Published 1993 by Prometheus Books

97 96 95 94 93   5 4 3 2 1

Library of Congress Cataloging-in-Publication Data

Stein, Gordon.
    The sorcerer of kings : the case of Daniel Dunglas Home and William
Crookes / Gordon Stein.
        p.   cm.
    Includes bibliographical references and index.
    ISBN 0-87975-863-5 (alk. paper)
    1. Home, D. D. (Daniel Dunglas), 1833–1886. 2. Crookes, William, Sir,
1832–1919. 3. Cook, Florence, 1856?–1904. 4. Parapsychology—Investigation—
History—19th century. 5. Mediums—Great Britain—History—19th
century. 6. Spiritualists—Great Britain—History—19th century. I. Title.
BF1283.H7S74   1993
133.9'1'092—dc20
[B]   93-23311
                                                              CIP

Printed in the United States of America on acid-free paper.

Contents

8   Contents

Foreword

I'm very pleased that Dr. Gordon Stein has put together such a definitive book on the spirit medium "still recognized as the finest physical medium of the nineteenth century," Daniel Dunglas Home, and the involvement of the very eminent scientist Sir William Crookes in examining Home's mediumship. Since this is the primary evidential case presented by believers for validation of spiritualistic claims, it needs to be carefully scrutinized.

Discussing whether Home really had supernatural powers or was simply a trickster is a little like discussing whether David Copperfield *really* can fly around the stage, or if it might be a trick. Wheel-spinning seems to occupy more folks than it should. Angels-on-the-head-of-a-pin would be a more useful subject in which to become involved. But the considerable prestige of Sir William cannot be ignored: he was well-educated, observant, and intelligent.

It has always seemed difficult for even the skeptics to believe that Crookes might have actually been deceived by tricks performed by Home, let alone by those used by Anna Eva Fay, Florence Cook, and the others he examined. My own personal experience with those individuals learned in science has shown me that they are sometimes even more easily duped than lesser-informed persons, especially when the matter under examination involves aspects of the personal needs and beliefs of the examiners. Also, since scientists employ logic in their consideration of matters which come to their attention, and the competent fraud is equipped to employ that fact against them, I find no difficulty in accepting that simple tricks could have fooled Crookes.

Similarly, I have no problem in considering the possibility, put forth strongly in this book, that Crookes might have actually, knowingly lent himself to the deception. He believed totally in the basic claims of spiritualism, such as survival after death, the ability of certain persons to facilitate communication between the two "worlds" they postulated, and other claimed phenomena that he felt could and should come to the attention of science. Tempering all that enthusiasm was the strong suspicion that dark forces other than departed persons might be the agents of the amazing things Crookes thought he experienced, and he preferred that explanation over the more spiritual one. Apparently, he also felt that it more closely satisfied his needs as a scientist.

Such an avid and capable observer and investigator as Dr. Eric J. Dingwall, who labored all of his ninety-plus years in pursuit of real, hard evidence for survival after death and never found it, was personally satisfied that Crookes was deceived, at least by Florence Cook. If that is so, and we do know that Crookes was convinced by others who were subsequently proven fraudulent or who confessed their fraud, Crookes's evidence in favor of Home is highly suspect.

Concerning Home as a competent performer, a valuable observation made here by Dr. Stein is that his major strength was not the physical techniques he employed, but the manipulation to which he subjected his witnesses and supporters. Home was always in control of the conditions under which he performed, in exactly the same way that a conjuror must be. The reconstructions of performances made by witnesses, as Stein points out, were incomplete, fuzzy, presumptuous, and often quite wrong, a situation that also holds with descriptions of conjuring tricks. Dates, sizes, locations, times, positions, and actual events were no better reported on by Crookes than by other spectators. He was no scientist when confronted with evidence he earnestly wanted to believe, and in fact needed to believe.

Upon losing his brother Phillip at an untimely age, Sir William Crookes did what many another intellectual has done: he embraced an unlikely but satisfying set of beliefs that removed from him the pain of the loss. Bishop James A. Pike, whose son Jim was a suicide at age twenty, went through a similar process in 1966, only to die miserably three years later while on a desert pilgrimage in Israel, searching for further evidence of his son's continued existence on the "other side." Sir Arthur Conan Doyle, whose son Kingsley and beloved brother Innes both died of pneumonia at early ages, avidly adopted spiritualism and devoted the rest of his life to promoting it among the public.

Home was a parasite extraordinaire. He lived handsomely on "the kindness of strangers" who became his devoted slaves. A small revelation here, a minor physical miracle there, and he further reinforced their loyalty. Crookes did not resist or escape his blandishments and flattery, and eventually accepted this Svengali as a most trusted friend.

Crookes didn't really want to find out the truth, if that truth would not fit his needs. He had the attitude often found among scientists that the human element is unimportant, and he trusted his own instincts concerning personalities. As a result of his enormous ego, Crookes could not even entertain the notion that he might have been deceived in any way. He believed, in common with so many other dupes, that he was far too smart to be fooled; in actuality, he was not smart enough to recognize that he was the perfect patsy.

Consider this fact: we have before us today examples of persons who perform *far* more convincing, *much* better, and more mind-boggling feats than anything that has ever been attributed to Daniel Dunglas Home. Harry Blackstone, David Copperfield, Paul Daniels, and a host of admitted tricksters float people about in the air, chop willing assistants into slices, vanish elephants, and even survive monstrous buzz saws while witnessed by literally millions of persons via television or close-up in a theater. Those witnesses can be Ph.D.s, geniuses, or any other variety of "smart folks," but unless they have a knowledge of trickery, they will not solve the mysteries presented before them. How, then, can we point to Crookes and his very faulted observational techniques as he applied them to Home, and thus conclude that Home was genuine?

Unfortunately, the principals in this drama are all very dead, unless we believe what they told us about never-never land. We cannot refer to them for verification or other information, and we must follow Dr. Stein's detective work carefully to sift out as much of the truth as we can get. The inevitable conclusion arrived at is that Sir William Crookes's validation of Daniel Dunglas Home's mediumistic powers is not acceptable. This book effectively demolishes the myth that has been for so long a seemingly dependable source of proof for a highly unlikely set of claims.

Gordon Stein has given us here an effective weapon in the battle against irrationality and nonsense. It is a battle that may never be won, but if the world is really doomed to wallow in superstition, pseudoscience, and folly, it will not be because people like our author did not try to enlighten us.

James Randi
Plantation, Florida
January 1993

Preface

Spiritualism, A Short Background

In order to understand the subject of this book, take a minute to read this short background about spiritualism. You will then understand what all the fuss was about that this book details. It is difficult to appreciate today how important spiritualism was at the time.

The mystery of what, if anything, happens after death has always been of great interest to humans. We seem to be the only species that can conceive of death and the possibility that there might be something after it. All sorts of imaginative scenarios of what "life after death" is like have been written, and often accepted as true.

In 1848 the Fox sisters, living near Rochester, New York, began modern spiritualism by producing a series of "raps" or "knocks," supposedly from the spirit world, through which communication could be maintained. The public's interest was captured and soon many other methods of communicating with the spirits were devised. Among these were planchettes (Ouija boards) and slate writing, in which messages in chalk were found on small sealed slate blackboards. Other ways included direct voice communication from the spirits through the medium, the manifestation of glowing hands that touched people, the appearance of objects (apports) having some meaning to specific people, spirit photographs, and finally the actual materialization of a part or whole of the deceased relative or friend.

Spiritualism spread rapidly both in Britain and the United States, with mediums setting up shop everywhere. These mediums ranged from the blatantly fake to the highly skilled conjuror to the possibly authentic. A large number of spiritualist publications were founded, which reported on the more impressive séances that had occurred. The average member of the public was impressed by them all, since the desire to contact dead

13

loved ones was very strong. Almost any image or voice, no matter how unclear or ambiguous, was recognized by someone as their dead child, brother or sister, mother or father. Gradually a number of the more skillful mediums became the modern equivalent of "superstars." The others were frequently exposed as fakes, although some remained in business even after an exposure. Among the superstars was Daniel Dunglas Home, still recognized as the finest physical medium of the nineteenth century. Florence Cook was also a star for a while, as was Anna Eva Fay.

Physical mediumship existed on a large scale until about 1925. One of the people largely responsible for the eventual decline of the physical medium was the magician Harry Houdini. His highly publicized exposures of fake mediums eventually soured people on them. Today, the only remnant of the physical medium remaining is the trance channeler, who is a pale imitation of the best physical mediums.

Scientists generally remained aloof from the phenomena of spiritualism, unwilling to attend séances or examine the phenomena under controlled conditions. A rare exception was William Crookes, a chemist and physicist, who was highly respected in nineteenth-century British science. Crookes was ridiculed by many of his fellow scientists for his five-year investigation of a number of important spiritualist mediums. This book is the story of that investigation, plus an analysis of what went wrong with it.

Acknowledgments

This book was made possible by the help of many people, and I would like to thank as many of them as possible. In England, I would like to thank Allen Wesencraft, Peter Meadows, Nick Clark-Lowes, Nicolas Barker, Guy Lyon Playfair, Sir Roy Kimber, Godfrey Waller, William Knight, and Kenneth Crookes. In the United States, I would like to thank James Randi, Marcello Truzzi, Jerome Clark, Martin Gardner, Ray Hyman, Robert Gutchen, Robert Weisbord, the late D. Scott Rogo, Judith Haughton, Vicki Burnett, Marie Rudd, and Susan Pavao.

The libraries I used were absolutely essential and uniformly helpful and courteous. I would especially like to thank the staffs of the Cambridge University Library, the British Library, the Society for Psychical Research, the University of London and its Harry Price Collection, the Library of Congress, the New York Public Library, the Brown University Library, the Boston Public Library, the Bibliothèque Nationale, the University of California at Los Angeles Library, the University of California at Berkeley Library, and the University of Rhode Island Library.

Introduction

Home, Crookes, and Cook

Daniel Dunglas Home (1833–1886) always pronounced his last name "Hume." He is remembered today only by those with an interest in spiritualism. As Frank Podmore said in *The Newer Spiritualism:* "No medium ever performed more remarkable feats or before witnesses so distinguished or competent. Further, Home stands alone amongst physical mediums in that he was never exposed in fraudulent practices."[1] Even so, why should we be interested in Home today?

First, the trance channeling of today is nothing but an extension of the work of the mediums of the last century. Its falsity or validity stands or falls with that of the physical mediums. Secondly, humans have always been concerned about death. The question of whether there is a life after death is one that still interests us, and one that has not yet been definitively answered. Finally, don't we all want to know if the effects mediums were able to produce, especially the really amazing ones, were due to trickery or really reflected some forces in the universe about which we still know little?

Spiritualist mediums no longer play much of a role in society, although a few still exist. Yet, in the latter half of the nineteenth century and the first few years of the twentieth, they were a widespread and important part of British and American daily life. Why was this so, and what caused the near total demise of the medium?

There is a larger issue here as well. As historian Jan Oppenheim says, many of the investigators of psychic phenomena working for the British Society for Psychical Research,

> although repudiating orthodox Christianity . . . longed to find some other
> basis for the ethical precepts they cherished and some reassurance that

17

all human suffering was not utterly devoid of purpose. Implicitly they sought to use science to disclose the inadequacies of a materialist world view, and to suggest how much of cosmic significance scientific naturalism failed to explain.[2]

While it is quite easy to dismiss the phenomena of Home and those of spiritualism in general as due to poor observation and credulity, the situation changes when the observer is a respected scientist. Indeed, much of the validation of the genuineness of Home's phenomena rests upon the fact that Sir William Crookes, the famous British chemist, examined Home's phenomena under scientific conditions, and confirmed their authenticity. Much the same can be said of the full-body materializations of Florence Cook, which were again confirmed by Crookes. Although Crookes's investigations of both Home and Cook occupied only the period from 1870 to 1875—a small part of Crookes's scientific career (he died in 1919)—those examinations, at least as far as Home's phenomena are concerned, represented the closest those phenomena have ever come to scientific examination.

Crookes's expertise as a scientist is not open to question. His motivation to investigate spiritualistic phenomena is also fairly clear: He wanted to see if he could contact his recently deceased brother, Phillip. What is not clear is whether there were other "pressures" upon him, some of which he might not have consciously realized, that compromised his objectivity as a scientist.

If Crookes is shown to have been compromised, his testimony as to the genuineness of Home's phenomena is suspect and must be discarded. If that were to happen, there is little testimony of comparable scientific worth that could be substituted. In effect, the scientific validation of Home's phenomena, crude as that validation may be by our present-day standards, sinks or swims with the investigation by William Crookes. That is why so much of the present work is devoted to an examination of Crookes's work on Home and Florence Cook.

Trevor Hall has suggested in his book *The Medium and the Scientist*[3] that Crookes was having an affair with Florence Cook. Crookes's pronouncements of the genuineness of Florence's phenomena were, according to Hall, simply a payoff to her for being his mistress. The "investigation" of her by Crookes was a cover for the continuation of their romance. Whatever the truth or falsity of this explanation may be (and it will be examined in detail), it would seem to fail when we try to use a similar relationship to explain Crookes's involvement with Home.

Whenever we try to explain how something has occurred, we use reason and logic, plus an understanding of the basic physical laws of nature to frame our explanation. What if we simply omit several key facts in our explanation? Usually that will cause the explanation to seem inadequate. Many cases of "mysterious" phenomena, such as ships vanishing in the Bermuda Triangle, are made mysterious by the omission, intentional or not, of some key data. When the missing data are supplied, the mystery vanishes, and a natural, prosaic explanation suffices (e.g., the plane ran out of fuel in a severe storm). Perhaps some of the reported phenomena of spiritualism only seem to be mysterious because some facts have been omitted.

After reading Home's *Incidents in My Life* (First Series),[4] one's mind reels. Either there are spirits of the dead that are potential visitors of the living (in which case many world views will have to be severely revised), or some enormous fraud has been cleverly perpetrated upon a large number of people. Which of these is more likely to be the case?

I have examined the various theoretical possibilities involved here. They can be summarized as follows: Either spiritualism is true, and Home's manifestations genuine, or spiritualism is false, and Home's manifestations also false. If spiritualism is true, it seems odd and improbable that the spirits of the dead would make themselves known to the living by tapping on tables, moving furniture around, playing on the accordion, and tying knots in handkerchiefs.

If spiritualism is false, there are two possibilities: either Home was *consciously* aware of the fraudulent nature of his phenomena (in which case he was a conjuror), or he was naive and was not consciously trying to fool anyone. In the latter case, we are left with the difficult task of explaining how the phenomena occurred. They may, perhaps, be natural phenomena misinterpreted by the viewers.

My personal position on this matter is as follows: Home was either a *conscious* fraud, or spiritualism is true. If spiritualism is true, then how do we account for the following two sets of facts? (1) Many mediums have been exposed as fraudulent. If spirits really existed, as claimed, there would be no need for fraud. (2) Since the heyday of spiritualism ended about 1930 (i.e., sixty years ago), the spirits have been strangely silent. They also were silent before 1850. Have they no longer any desire to communicate with living people? For these two reasons, plus my personal knowledge of conjuring techniques, I have come to the conclusion (inevitable, it seems to me) that Daniel Dunglas Home was a *conscious* fraud, and a conjuror. True, he was an extremely clever and original conjuror. Nevertheless, I think I have been able to explain how all of his effects were produced, using strictly conjuring explanations. In doing so, I have had to reveal a number of magicians' secrets, but I hope that my fellow magicians will forgive me for doing so. The vast majority of the effects in question are no longer performed, and a knowledge of how Home did his effects will produce far more good, it seems to me, than the revealing of them will produce harm to professional conjurors.

At this point, one critical piece of information needs to be mentioned. It is in answer to the question of why no conjuror has previously been able (or willing) to explain Home's illusions. I think it is because (1) almost no conjuror (with one or two exceptions to be discussed later) *personally* witnessed Home's performances. Home was very selective about whom he allowed to attend his séances, and, since they were free, he felt he could decide who could attend. (2) Most of those who have attempted to explain *what was reported* by eyewitnesses who were not conjurors have forgotten a very simple fact: Conjuring is the art of fooling people into thinking that they have experienced something that they really have not experienced. For example, the magician who makes his audience *think* that he has sawed a woman in two, and then restored her, has fooled the audience into so thinking.

Actually, the woman was not sawed in half, yet most of the audience would swear that they saw her cut in two. This malobservation is probably at work in the eyewitness descriptions of Home's effects as well. If we remember this, much of our former inability to explain his effects disappears. Of course, what Home did *in reality* must produce an *impression* upon the observer that is similar to what has been claimed to have been observed.

Of course, there is a danger inherent in this position. It is easy to dismiss *all* of Home's more clever phenomena as simply due to poor observation. This will not do, and I will not take this easy way out. Every time a phenomenon of Home is discussed (and I will try to discuss them all), an explanation of what Home probably *did* that caused his audience to observe what they reported seeing will be given. The phenomena actually produced by Home may, of course, not be those "seen" by his audience.

Home never charged for admission to his séances, yet he lived quite well. This happened because he was a shrewd politician. He curried favor in high places, always making sure that royalty, diplomats, politicians, lawyers, and physicians were among the audience "allowed" to attend. As a result of his high sociability and impressive phenomena, word soon spread throughout Europe that Home was a person worth getting to know, and the aristocracy was clamoring to attend his séances. Home was invited to stay in the homes of some of the wealthiest people, and was given valuable jewelry as gifts. The fact that many of his séances were performed right in the houses of his audience gave a great deal of confidence, probably misplaced, to the participants that nothing could be "rigged." As preventing the audience from suspecting that trickery was being perpetrated removes a great deal of the need to conceal that trickery, this greatly added to Home's apparent rate of success. In addition, the few times he *was* caught cheating, the guests chose to ignore it and said nothing publicly. Thus, to this day, you will see the statement made about Home in the more popular literature that he was never caught in fraud. What really happened was that he was never publicly exposed as a fraud, although he was caught cheating several times, as will be seen.

Home was protected from exposure by the power of his friends. That is not to suggest that they thought him a fraud, but rather that they thought him genuine and were loyal enough to defend him from criticism, even when that criticism was justified. True, the few times there is a record of his being caught in an apparent deception, it seems pretty clear that deception on his part was the only possible explanation for what was reported. This assumes the truthfulness of the witnesses against Home, which may or may not be a good assumption.

For example, one time Home was caught with a small vial that he was examining. He quickly abandoned the vial upon noticing that he had been observed. The vial was picked up by someone who had observed Home, and its contents were analyzed. The substance turned out to be what was then called "oil of phosphorus." We now know this as olive oil in which as much white phosphorous as will dissolve after several weeks has been allowed to dissolve. The properties of this interesting liquid, which will be discussed later, make it suited to only one purpose, namely producing lights or glowing forms in the dark. As the production of these glowing forms was, at least for a while, a feature of Home's séances, it is difficult to guess what Home would be doing with a vial of this oil unless he were experimenting with its use in sittings. That, of course, would be an indication that Home used deception in his séances.

Home's career and reputation suffered a major public setback when a British court ruled in the case of *Lyon* v. *Home* that Home had used undue influence to make wealthy widow Jane Lyon accept Home as her "son," and turn over to him more than forty thousand pounds (then $200,000). The judge ordered the money to be returned to Mrs. Lyon. The case made quite a stir at the time, and Home's loss in court *could* have dealt the death blow to the future success of his mediumship. Yet it did not have much of a long-term effect upon Home's popularity among the wealthy. There were a number of defenses of Home's behavior published at the time. Part of these defenses was due to the fact that Home's supporters were convinced of the genuineness of his phenomena, although if the lawsuit had questioned Home's phenomena *directly,* it might have hurt "business" more.

Florence Cook was a full-form materializing medium, whom Crookes also tested for genuineness and pronounced authentic. She was another important figure in the history of spiritualism. However, unlike Home, she was publicly caught in fraud a number of times and denounced publicly. These instances will be discussed, as will her role in evaluating the worth of Crookes's own observations and writings about spiritualist mediums.

I have made some assumptions in this book, which I believe are all justified:

- I have assumed that D. D. Home and Mrs. Home's retelling of his séances, which have nearly always been picked up from published accounts by attendees and from letters by participants, are honest reports of what these attendees thought they saw. I do not think that any of these accounts was invented or intentionally falsified. I have checked the contents of Home's and Mrs. Home's books against the actual letters in a number of cases, and I have always found that the letters were quoted accurately. Frederic W. H. Myers checked the letters against the books in Paris in 1889, and came to the same conclusion.

- In connection with the above, when either of the Homes included accounts of events, I am assuming that they tried to put the best light upon what was reported by others, perhaps by judicious, but not unethical, editing. Many of the negative reports on Home are reprinted in the Homes' books, but with statements by the Homes (or others) vindicating D. D. Home.

- I have assumed that the criticisms of Home that are addressed in their books by either of the Homeses are the ones that are most easily disposed of by a presentation of the facts. Many erroneous and frivolous charges were made against D. D. Home. Surely disposing of errors is a useful service, but not all charges made against Home are ever addressed. I assume that the ones remaining unanswered are the ones most difficult to answer.

- I have *not* assumed that Florence Cook and William Crookes had anything but a relationship as acquaintances. I will let the facts speak for themselves as to whether anything more was involved.

Although not widely known, there were instances where D. D. Home was publicly accused of cheating. I will discuss each of these instances in detail later, but for now let's just call them (1) the phosphorylated oil vial incident, (2) the bare foot under the table incident, (3) the sculptured human hands report, (4) the false appendages attached to his shoulder report, (5) the "Lizzie"/"Eliza" fraud, and (6) the harmonica report. Without going into details about any of these incidents now, it can be said in general that if *any* of these is *true,* it casts serious doubt upon the genuineness of *all* of Home's phenomena. If Home was genuine, he did not need to resort to trickery, and each of the six reports above, if true, was a case of blatant trickery. On the other hand, if none of these reports can be substantiated, and if there are no additional reports of a similar nature, then Home can truely be said to have never been caught in a fraud.

I must at this point take up the idea that a medium, or other producer of paranormal phenomena, could be *sometimes* fraudulent yet *sometimes* genuine. After much thought about this, I confess that I am somewhat puzzled as to *why* anyone would take the position that a medium who has been caught in fraud might still produce genuine phenomena at least some of the time. The best argument that I have heard in favor of this position was put to me by Guy Lyon Playfair in a personal discussion. He said that a medium is basically a performer, and that people expect a performance. If that performance cannot be produced by genuine means on a given occasion, the medium may have to resort to fraud to avoid disappointing the audience. While this may occasionally be the case, I think that in the vast majority of cases, an *honest person who was capable of producing genuine phenomena* would simply say that he or she were not in good form on those occasions when this was true, and leave the audience disappointed. Of course, a *dishonest* person would do as Playfair suggests, but then how can we trust this type of person's word about when he or she is producing *genuine* phenomena? I would rather deal only with those who have never been caught in fraud, and disqualify all others as fraudulent.

A part of the problem that any investigator of Home's phenomena has to deal with is the "help" that has already been given by other writers about Home. Much of what they say is simply untrue, even by D. D. Home and his wife's own standards of what occurred. I am not advocating that everything that the Homes' books said was what actually happened, but rather that more modern writers should at least quote accurately from the reports given by the Homes or others.

An example of someone who has muddied up the waters is Lynn Picknett in her 1987 book *Flights of Fancy?*[5] While this book is right in calling our attention to Home and Florence Cook, it adopts a highly credulous attitude toward their phenomena. This would be forgivable if the phenomena were correctly described, but they often are not. Picknett says, for example, that "Home was requested very firmly to leave the Eternal City [Rome], never to float about its portals again" (p. 21). Home was never reported or recorded as levitating in Rome, and the request to leave came from the pope himself, in an effort to discourage popular acceptance of "sorcery." She also names Maurice Davies as Charles, and Jane Lyon as Lyons. These are simple facts that anyone can check. Perhaps worst of all is her refusal to entertain any thought that Home's or Cook's phenomena could be anything other than exactly what people reported to have seen. This attitude I find as bad as that of the most closed-minded of skeptics.

Elizabeth Jenkins's *The Shadow and the Light: A Defence of Daniel Dunglas Home the Medium*[6] requires a few special comments. Miss Jenkins says in her Introduction that she has relied upon D. D. Home's two autobiographical volumes and upon Madame Home's two biographical volumes, plus some additional material about *Lyon* v. *Home* and about the Browning séance. Miss Jenkins feels the need to defend Home against two previous and somewhat hostile biographies, Horace Wyndham's *Mr. Sludge, the Medium*[7] and Jean Burton's *Heyday of a Wizard.*[8] If all she has relied upon are the four books mentioned, all of which have an understandably pro-Home bias, then it is no wonder that she feels the need to defend Home. It would indeed appear that Home's memory has been treated unfairly if all that is utilized as sources of the facts are what Miss Perkins says she used.

In contrast, I have tried to examine *everything* that in any way dealt with Home or Cook. This, in addition to the D. D. Home papers themselves, has included all published studies of Home, Crookes, Cook, or any of the mediums Crookes studied. I have been greatly aided in this task by the presence of Eric J. Dingwall's encyclopedic card files now at the Harry Price Library of the University of London, and by the Crookes and Medhurst files from the Society for Psychical Research, now at Cambridge University. Dingwall's files contain bibliographic information about every reference he managed to uncover about Home or Cook in more than seventy-five years of active research. They are well-organized and invariably error-free, as far as I have been able to determine. The Crookes file, compiled by R. George Medhurst and Kathleen Mollie Goldney, and Medhurst's own files contain the results of their many years of investigation of Trevor Hall's work on Crookes and Florence Cook.

I have also had the opportunity to carefully inspect the scrapbooks compiled by Trevor Hall for his books on Home, Crookes, and Cook. They are among the Dingwall scrapbooks in the Harry Price Library. The contents of Dingwall's own scrapbooks have also produced much of value on Home and Crookes. The Blackburn correspondence with the Cooks has also been utilized, although the closing of the Britten Library in Manchester, which formerly housed the letters, has meant that the originals, now in storage at the British Spiritualist Union Library in Stansted, have become inaccessible. I have relied upon typescripts prepared by

Goldney and Medhurst, and have compared these with the typescripts prepared by Trevor Hall. In almost every case in which a letter was quoted in a book as coming from the spiritualist press or elsewhere, I have gone back to the magazine itself to verify the text. Where this was not possible, I have relied upon the transcripts made by Goldney and Medhurst.

While some of the reasoning I have employed in this book is not original, much of it has never been applied to Home's phenomena before. What I am referring to is the conjuror's-eye view of things. If we can demonstrate that *all* of the perceived phenomena claimed for Home could have been done by conjuring with virtually no complex equipment, we may have the answer to a mystery that has intrigued people for more than one hundred years. If we cannot so demonstrate, then the mystery remains. Yet Sir William Crookes, in his daring (for a Victorian scientist) investigations of Home and Florence Cook, changes greatly in our estimation, depending upon how the phenomena turn out to have been produced. Crookes's reputation lies in the balance.

Finally, it will pay us to keep in mind a warning by William S. Sadler that the séance room is exactly the *wrong* environment necessary to conduct scientific studies of mediums.[9] This is true because of (1) the usual absence of light, (2) the lack of control over conditions being allowed, (3) the diversion of attention by the medium, (4) the element of surprise on the part of the medium, (5) the possibility of concealment in the room, (6) the power of suggestion by the medium, and (7) the emotional expectancy on the part of the sitters.

Part One

Florence Cook
The Medium

1

Biographical Sketch of Florence Cook

Florence Eliza Cook was born 3 June 1856 at Cobham, England, the daughter of Henry Cook, a printer, and Emma Cook. This information was long shrouded in mystery, with the claim made that the birth was never registered.[1] However, the birth *was* registered (#441 for 1856 in the subdistrict of Northfleet, Kent [North Aylesford district]). The importance of the date of birth of Florence Cook has to do with exactly how old she was when she first met William Crookes. It turns out that she was then seventeen when Crookes first met her in 1873.

What is known about Florrie Cook's career before age seventeen is sketchy. We do know that she was dismissed from a teaching post in early January 1872 because her spiritualistic activities were giving or threatening to give the school that employed her a bad name. She soon joined up with Frank Herne, a professional spiritualist medium and later of Herne and Williams. This association may have begun as early as 1871, and lasted through December 1873.[2] Florrie also worked as a medium with Mrs. Bassett and with Mr. and Mrs. Nelson Holmes.

The types of phenomena produced at séances gradually evolved. Florrie Cook's specialty soon became full-figure materializations, which meant the production of the entire body of a "spirit" that would then move about the room and talk with the people present. As early as 1871, there were American reports of spirit hands and faces inside the medium's cabinet. The first British medium to produce materializations in her séances seems to have been Mrs. Guppy in early 1872.[3] During this séance, a small face, "white as alabaster," appeared at an opening in the cabinet at the same time that the faces of the medium and her associate also appeared at other openings in the cabinet. In April 1872 Herne and Williams began to add materializations to their séances. These seem to have been the first

British séances in which forms and faces left the cabinet and moved about the darkened room. Florence Cook, however, seems to have been the first British medium to produce full-form materializations that left the cabinet in good light.

The full-form materialization was not without its dangers, however. Several times the materialization was seized by spectators at the séance. Florence's career as a medium could have been ended with each of these exposures. Instead, she managed to stay in business, although she outlived her earlier fame, and was able for a long time to retire from active mediumship. In her last few years, when she moved away from living with the rest of the family, she was reduced to near poverty. After William Crookes stopped testing her in May 1874, her Katie King materializations were replaced with one called "Marie."

From that point onward, Florence seems to have shared in the good fortune of her sister Kate Salina Cook, who was able to pry large sums of money from wealthy businessman Charles Blackburn. Florence had married ship captain Edward Elgie Corner in April of 1874. The Corners and the rest of the Cook family moved over the next twenty-five years into a series of fine houses. They were fairly well-to-do. Only Captain Corner seems to have worked regularly. Florence Cook stopped working regularly as a medium. Her sister Kate Salina Cook *did* produce her materialization, called "Lillie Gordon," regularly. It was Kate who had convinced Charles Blackburn to give them continuous financial support, including eventually a legacy to enable the Cooks to take care of Blackburn's mentally unstable daughter Eliza. When Charles Blackburn died in 1891, he left additional money for the Cooks, the Corners, and the care of Eliza. Eliza died in 1921.

After Florence died in 1904, Edward Corner married her sister Kate in 1907, shortly after such marriages were made legal in England. Kate died in 1923, and Edward Corner in 1928. Corner died rather wealthy, and seems to have been the final repository of much of Charles Blackburn's money. Upon Corner's death, his estate was divided between his two daughters by Florence Cook, both of whom then lived in South America.[4]

This background gives us a perspective that may prove valuable, as Nelson Holmes and Frank Herne were later exposed as frauds. Herne was caught with fake spirit photographs.[5] He was also caught in December 1875 impersonating "John King."[6] Holmes was exposed in America.[7] This exposure was based upon the confession of an assistant who *may* not have been telling the truth.

2

The Phenomena of Florence Cook

On 21 April 1872 Florence Cook and Frank Herne held a joint séance at Hackney. The mediums sat in the dark. Florence and Herne went into her curtained-off corner of the room, called the cabinet, and soon after a figure appeared entirely covered in drapery, including the face. The figure rushed over to Mr. Cook, Florence's father, and grabbed his shoulders, shaking him and calling him "Cookey" in the voice of Florence's spirit guide, "Katie King." John King—a spirit who was Katie King's father in early history, although both were now long dead—then came out of the cabinet, also completely covered with drapery. He shook hands with the sitters, and both he and Katie left the room. The importance of all this is that it marked the first time Florrie Cook had produced a full-figure materialization. It was a process that Florrie would gradually perfect, claiming that she had to "grow in strength" before she could produce a more complete physical materialization.

Soon Florrie was producing perfect full-form materializations of Katie King. These were so complete that only the hair was covered with a type of shawl, while a normal robe covered the rest of the body. This Katie was also physical enough to be touched, have her hand held, and pulse taken.

On 9 December 1873 William Volckman, who had gained admittance to the séance only with great difficulty, observed the figure of Katie King for forty minutes. By then he was convinced that she was being impersonated by Florrie Cook. Finally, he grabbed the "spirit." In the struggle that followed, the very much physical Katie finally got away with the help of several of the gentlemen sitters, and rushed back into the cabinet. About five minutes later, when an investigation was finally made of the cabinet, Florrie Cook was found in a dishevelled condition, but still tied with the same tape with which she had originally been bound.[1]

Trevor Hall has suggested that Charles Blackburn, the wealthy man who had been supporting Florrie so that she could give séances, was angry at this exposure and threatened to cut off his support.[2] Hall has also suggested that Florrie, in desperation, threw herself upon William Crookes's mercy.[3] That, Hall suggests, was how Crookes first became involved with Florrie Cook in any way but as an observer at her séances. However, Medhurst and Goldney have suggested that Hall's interpretation is faulty.[4] They point out that Mr. Volckman was working for the rival medium Mrs. Guppy, whom he later married. They quote from a letter dated 16 September 1876 from the medium Nelson Holmes to D. D. Home, in which Holmes reveals that Mrs. Guppy was furious with Florrie Cook for having taken away much of Mrs. Guppy's business. Mrs. Guppy, Holmes says, had planned to employ a couple of people to go to a Cook séance and throw acid in the face of the medium. Such a plot was never carried out, but Mr. Volckman was to have been involved. It thus seems likely that Mr. Volckman's behavior in grabbing Katie King had been planned in advance, and was not a spur-of-the-moment idea, as he had claimed.

Medhurst and Goldney also cite a letter from Mr. Blackburn quoted by W. H. Harrison in *The Spiritualist* of 6 February 1874.[5] Although two months after the Volckman incident, Blackburn makes it clear that he intends to continue financial support of Florrie, but only at séances from which the public has been excluded, and with only "scientific men" admitted. Although this *might* have removed the fear on Florence's part that her financial support had ended, the fact that two months had passed since the grabbing incident may reveal that Blackburn's decision to continue support had not come easily.

According to Medhurst and Goldney, Crookes had not attended any of Florence Cook's séances before December 1873,[6] but Crookes's own letter register (the letters themselves are lost), reproduced in Fournier d'Albe's biography of Crookes,[7] shows that letters were received by Crookes from Florrie Cook inviting him to attend séances in May and September of *1872*. That would be, of course, *before* the Volckman incident. Although the entries in Crookes's letter register are not totally clear, it *is* apparent that Crookes never discussed in print or in an existing letter anything that happened at a séance with Florrie Cook before December 1873. The notes by Crookes of this séance, published in *The Spiritualist* for 19 December 1873, are worth reproducing at length. They show quite well Crookes's early attitude toward Florrie's materializations.

> Spirit Forms—Miss Cook has been very ill and nervous since the outrage printed in the last number of this journal, but last Tuesday night was well enough to give a séance to a large and influential company of friends,

at the residence of Mr. J. C. Luxmoore, J.P., 16 Gloucester-square, Hyde-Park, W. Neither she nor her friends entered the dark room to be used as a cabinet before the séance began, and all the gentlemen present, including Mr. W. Crookes, F.R.S., searched it. There being a second door to the room, a short piece of thick wire was passed through the keyhole, after the door was locked, and pieces of thick metal soldered to the opposite end of the wire, thus upsetting any theory that a person could get in with a duplicate key. The window was firmly secured in many ways. All the ladies of the party, including, among others, Mrs. Honywood, Mrs. Crookes and Mrs. Tappan, searched the medium in a bedroom before she entered the séance room, where she was bound and tied down as usual, and the knots sealed with the signet ring of Mr. Crookes. Katie came out in flowing white robes and bare feet, in the usual way, and wherever the white robes came from, it is certain that they did not get into the séance room by any method known to any living mortal. The knots and seals were intact after Katie retired.[8]

On at least one occasion Florence Cook's Katie King paraded around Crookes's laboratory arm in arm with Mary Rosina Showers's materialization named "Florence Maple." Serjeant Cox wrote of this incident in a letter, the relevant portion of which follows:

I have seen the forms of "Katie" and "Florence" together in the full light, coming out from the room in which Miss Cook and Miss Showers were placed, walking about, talking, playing girlish tricks, patting us and pushing. They were solid flesh and blood and bone. They breathed, and perspired, and ate, and wore a white head-dress and a white robe from neck to foot, made of cotton and woven by a loom. Not merely did they resemble their respective mediums, they were facsimilies of them—alike in face, hair, complexion, teeth, eyes, hands, and movements of the body. Unless he had been otherwise so informed, no person would have doubted for a moment that the two girls who had been placed behind the curtains were now standing *in propria persona* before the curtain playing very prettily the character of ghost.

On that occasion there was nothing to avoid this conclusion but the bare assertion of the forms in white that they were not what they appeared to be, but two other beings in the likeness of Miss Cook and Miss Showers; and that the real ladies were at that moment asleep on the sofa behind the curtain. But of this their assertion no proof whatever was given or offered or permitted. The fact might have been established in a moment beyond all doubt by the simple process of opening the curtain and exhibiting the two ladies then and there upon the sofa, wearing their black gowns. But this only certain evidence was not proffered, nor, indeed, was it allowed us—the conditions exacted from us being that we should do nothing by which, if it were a trick, we should be enabled to discover it.

This and similar exhibitions have been advanced as proofs of positive materialization, and it is said, "You have seen, heard, touched the spirit forms." True, I have seen two forms, and they were material forms beyond all question. But they exactly resembled the ladies, and not the slightest proof was given or allowed to me that they were not the ladies themselves, as they appeared to all of us to be.

But I have had one piece of evidence that goes far to throw a doubt over the whole. At a sitting with Miss Showers a few days ago, the curtain behind which the form of Florence [Maple] was exhibiting her face, was opened by a spectator ignorant of the conditions, and a peep behind the scenes was afforded to those present. I am bound, in the interests of truth and science, to say that I, as well as all the others, beheld revealed to us, not a form in front and a lady in the chair, but the chair empty, and the lady herself at the curtain wearing the ghost head-dress, and dressed in her own black gown! Nor was she lying on the floor as some have surmised. When the head was thrust out between the curtain the eyes were turned up with the fixed stare which has been observed in the supposed Florence [Maple], but the eyes rapidly assumed their natural position when the exposure was made, and the hands were forthwith actively employed in trying to close the curtain, and in the struggle with the inspecting lady the spirit head-dress fell off. I was witness to it all, and the extraordinary scene that followed—the voice crying out "You have killed my medium!"—an alarm which, by the bye, was quite needless, for she was neither killed or injured beyond the vexation of the discovery. She said in excuse that she was unconscious of what she had done, being in a state of trance.[9]

3

Florence's Joint Séances

Florence Cook sometimes worked with Mary Rosina Showers. Miss Rosina Showers later admitted that she herself was a fraud. She was tested by Crookes over a period of time in 1874. Among the tests that Miss Showers failed were such simple things as having her hands dipped into a bowl of dye before being tied in the cabinet, and seeing whether the hands of the "spirit" were also dyed (they were).[1] Why such a test was never done on Florence Cook is quite puzzling, as it is so simple and so difficult to circumvent. It is implied in a letter from Lord Rayleigh to his mother on 3 May 1874 that this test *was* done on Florrie Cook by Crookes, and that she passed,[2] but Crookes never mentions it himself. Several people claim to have seen Miss Showers and her materialization together at the same time. Among these people were Mr. Luxmoore, one of the most credulous of all the spiritualists of the time, and Florrie Cook!

Rosina Showers's exposure came in the form of a purported confession she made to Annie (Anna) Eva Fay, another medium who was later exposed as a fake. The confession is described by Crookes to Daniel Dunglas Home in a letter dated 3 November 1875, and quoted in Medhurst and Goldney. This letter is so important both at this point and later in our inquiry that it is reproduced in full below:

Private
                                             Nov. 3rd, 1875
                                             20 Mornington Road
                                             London, N.W.

My Dear Dan,
      Absence from home has prevented me from replying to your letter of the 30th ult. by return of post.

35

I do not know what reports you may have heard about me, and I wish you would as a friend tell me more of them, and if possible send me one of the letters you say refers to me. I think I know the originator of the reports. Were the letters not written to Mr. Gledstanes?

As for Miss Showers, the facts are simple enough. She confessed to Mrs. Fay that her manifestations were all a trick, and very properly Mrs. Fay told me. I thereupon employed Mrs. Fay, as I should employ a detective to unearth a fraud, and by her assistance got a complete confession in Miss S.'s handwriting. I have since had several interviews with Miss S. and have induced her to give up these tricks, I promising not to bring about a public exposure but only to warn my private friends. Do not therefore say anything about this.

Mrs. Showers found out I was meeting her daughter and fired up at it, putting the worst construction on it. I was bound by promise not to expose Miss S. to her mother, so I refused to explain. Probably I was wrong in this, but I could not break a promise.

But Miss S. had accomplices according to her account, and one of the gentlemen implicated has before now written very shameful things about me to Paris, so between the Mother and others I am getting the reputation of a Don Juan. Fortunately those whose opinion I care about, know me too well to believe these slanders, but it is very annoying, for I cannot appeal to the law for a remedy in this case, knowing the very great injury which the cause of truth would suffer if so impudent a fraud were to be publicly exposed in the newspapers. My good and true wife knows *everything* about this and quite approves of my conduct, so I can well afford to let the matter blow over.

I have worked hard and sacrificed more than anyone would believe for the cause of spiritualism, and I have met with little but calumny, slander, backbiting and abuse from spiritualists. To anyone else I would not take the trouble to make these explanations, but I look upon you as one of the real friends I have, and I would not spare any trouble to retain your friendship and good opinion. If you want any further explanation ask and I will send it you, but please consider what I tell you as given in confidence.

My wife sends her love to Julie and yourself, and with the same from me, Believe me,

Your affectionate friend,
WILLIAM CROOKES[3]

Crookes's letter of 6 November 1875 to Home is also important:

Private   November 6th, 1875
                                              20 Mornington Road
                                              London, N.W.

My dear Dan,

As Miss Showers begged so earnestly that I would not expose her
to her mother and it was necessary for me to see her several times, I
had to write occasional notes to her making appointments. I put nothing
in them that all the world might not know. But I have a letter from
Mrs. Showers in which she cooly tells me that she intercepted *every* letter,
opened them by ungumming the envelopes over hot water and replaced
my note by one written by herself imitating my writing. More than this
she tells me she has written to her daughter—purporting to come from
me—when I had not written at all. Miss Showers at last showed me
one of these forgeries; neither the language nor the writing was mine.
Of course I cannot say how far the woman may have gone in these
forgeries, with the object of damaging my character, but she dare not
do more than threaten, for my writing is too well know [sic] to deceive
anyone I care about. We saw Carrie a few days ago. She sends her
love to you and your wife. Accept the same from Nellie and myself,

                              Yours very sincerely,
                              WILLIAM CROOKES[4]

Both letters are of such a personal and intimate character, especially
for the 1870s, that they also shed light on the nature of the relationship
between Crookes and Home.

At present, the information in those letters about Miss Showers can
probably be taken as trustworthy. *Why* Rosina Showers would confess to
Mrs. Fay, who did *not* do materializations until after 1875,[5] is a matter of
conjecture. Whether Mrs. Fay asked as a matter of professional curiosity
how the materializations were done, or whether Mrs. Fay was asked by Crookes
or others to pry this information from Miss Showers, no one can now tell.

The actual confession of Miss Showers also seems to have disappeared,
probably destroyed after Crookes's death by his family with the bulk of
his papers on spiritualism. However, Trevor Hall points out a letter dated
8 March 1876 (i.e., five months after the Crookes/Home letters just cited)
from Serjeant Cox to D. D. Home. The letter was reproduced in Home's
book *Lights and Shadows of Spiritualism*. In the letter, Cox tells Home
that he has learned from a description written by one medium to another
who desired instruction, how "the trick" (i.e., full-form materialization)
is done and then describes it. Medhurst and Goldney feel that this description can only have come from Miss Showers's confession. Perhaps, and
if so, it is worth reproducing the relevant part of the letter here:

But I have learned how the trick is done. I have seen the description of it given by a medium to another medium who desired instruction. The letter was in her own handwriting, and the whole style of it showed it to be genuine.

She informs her friend that she comes to the séance prepared with a dress that is easily taken off with a little practice. She says it may be done in two or three minutes. She wears two shifts (probably for warmth). She brings a muslin veil of thin material (she gives its name, which I forget). *It is carried in her drawers!* It can be compressed into a small space, although when spread it covers the whole person. A pocket-handkerchief pinned round the head keeps back the hair. She states that she takes off all her clothes except the two shifts, and is covered by the veil. The gown is spread carefully upon the sofa over the pillows. In this array she comes out. She makes very merry with the spiritualists whom she thus gulls, and her language about them is anything but complimentary.

This explains the whole business. The question so often asked before was—where the robe could be carried? It could not be contained in the bosom or in a sleeve. Nobody seems to have thought of the drawers.

But it will be asked how we can explain the fact that some persons have been permitted to go behind the curtain when the form was before it, and have asserted that they saw or felt the medium. I am sorry to say the confession to which I have referred states without reserve that those persons knew it was a trick, and lent themselves to it. I am, of course, reluctant to adopt such a formidable conclusion, although the so-called "confession" was a confidential communication from one medium to another medium who had asked to be instructed how the trick was done. I prefer to adopt the more charitable conclusion that they were imposed upon, and it is easy to find how this was likely to be. The same suspicious precautions against detection were always adopted. The favoured visitor was an assured friend; one who, if detecting trickery, would shrink from proclaiming the cheat. But one was permitted to enter. A light was not allowed. There was nothing but the "darkness visible" of the lowered gas rays struggling through the curtain. I have noted that no one of them was ever permitted to see the face of the medium. It was always "wrapped in a shawl." The hands felt a dress, and imagination did the rest. The revealer of the secret above referred to says that, when she took off her gown to put on the white veil, she spread it upon the sofa or chair with pillows or something under it and this was what they felt and took for her body!

The lesson to be learned from all this is that no phenomena should be accepted as genuine that are not produced under strict test conditions. Investigators should be satisfied with no evidence short of the very best that the circumstances will permit. Why accept the doubtful testimony of one person groping in the dark when the question can be decided beyond dispute once and for ever by the simple process of drawing back the curtain while the alleged spirit is outside and showing the medium inside to the eyes of all present?[6]

Cox's hardheaded approach to the materializations did not end here. He saw readily how much of a logical trap lay in assuming that a materialization of a spirit could feel physically real, right down to having a pulse and a growling stomach. He states:

[The materialization] is no phantom, not even the crust of a human form, but it is a perfect human body, having as far as the senses can show us, all the shape and organ and functions of a woman. It has flesh, and bones, and hair, and nails, and saliva, and blood and veins and a beating heart, and a perspiring skin. Moreover it has a brain and a nerve structure obedient to that brain. And that brain is an educated brain, and has received an English education, for it converses in English. Nor does the wonder end here. It has learned to play the piano, which is a mechanical as well as an intellectual performance, only to be acquired by practice. This form talks the language of our time, plays and sings, jests and is quick at repartee. Talking involves the possession of the entire apparatus needful to that process: hence, though we cannot see or feel them, we know that there must be lungs and the complicated mechanism of the trachea, and this implies blood and blood implies a heart and muscles to move it, and nerves to set the muscles in action. It is a solid form, for Mr. Crookes has more than once, by permission, put his arm around its waist, and it was a warm, womanly form, with feelings, for it kisses and is kissed.[7]

Cox goes on to say that although it appears to be human by every criterion known, spiritualists say that it is no human being at all, but a spirit that presents itself in perfect human form. Cox says that this is "an astounding answer, not to be accepted on any mere assertion, and the amazed spectator demands proof of it, and the obvious method of proof is by conclusive evidence—by which I mean the best evidence that can be given—that the fact, seemingly incredible as it is, is nevertheless true." Cox says that reason dictates that a simple test "under conditions that preclude deception by the medium" can and should be done. For example, the curtains to the cabinet might be lifted and then "all the spectators would then see the medium and the form [i.e., the body of the materialization] at the same moment, and it is equally easy to assure themselves that the medium is herself and no other." Cox stated that he could not find any evidence that this simple test had ever been applied. The fact that there was a body lying in the cabinet with a shawl covering the face did *not* prove, according to Cox, that it was Florence Cook lying there. In fact, Cox points out, the presence of the shawl is suggestive that Florence Cook is *not* lying there.[8]

Dingwall feels that Medhurst and Goldney are in error when they state that the medium referred to in Cox's letter as receiving the confession is Annie Eva Fay.[9] Dingwall thinks that it is more likely to have been Lottie Fowler.

Who, exactly, wrote the document quoted is only of importance if we are to consider whether Rosina Showers's "confession," as obtained by Annie Eva Fay, contained the same "modus operandi" for full-figure materializations as did the document quoted by Cox. If it did, then grave doubt is cast upon the genuineness of Florrie Cook's materializations, as she and Rosina Showers were joint "materializers" on at least one occasion.[10] Worse yet are the assurances of the medium quoted by Cox that those who were allowed behind the curtain during the séances "knew it was a trick" and were in on the deception. If so, then Crookes must have been "in on it." If the two "confessions" are *different* documents, then we still have no details about Rosina Showers's confession, and Crookes is off the hook, at least for now.

The exhibition involving Florence Maple and Katie King parading around together, arm in arm, can be located geographically with interesting ramifications.

> Now where was this exhibition staged and under whose auspices? This question has not been stressed by the defence but the answer is hardly reassuring. It was, in all probability, in Crookes's own house and it was he who, we may assume, had full control over the performance. Can any reasonable person really bring himself to believe that the refusal to permit the simple test proposed by Cox that the curtain be opened while the materializations were out of the cabinet to show the mediums still in the cabinet was not due to the fact that the performance was blatantly fraudulent and that Crookes knew that it was?[11]

Dingwall also points out that

> Now, since Mary [Showers] knew that Florence was also fraudulent why did she not confront Crookes with her knowledge and threaten him with exposure? This is not such a formidable difficulty as appears at first sight. Had she done so and succeeded, the resulting scandal would have involved herself and her family, Florence Cook and Crookes. But Crookes had, in one sense, the upper hand. He might have told Mary that if it was true that Florence was occasionally naughty and played silly tricks, but that he had absolute proof of her being capable of producing genuine

phenomena since Mary had failed to satisfy in those very tests where Florence had succeeded. . . . Crookes promised to be silent except to a few chosen friends who would also be silent. Mary promised to cease for a time, but broke her promise within a few months as I have said.[12]

When Mary Showers and Florrie Cook had their joint séance, either they both knew they were frauds and *also* knew that Crookes knew, or they were very bold in thinking Crookes a fool who would be deceived by their "ridiculous performance," Dingwall says.

If we are asked to think that Crookes really believed in all of this, it appears his modern defenders are reducing him almost to the level of an imbecile and denigrating him to a far greater degree than Mr. Hall has done. . . . Even if we assume that Crookes believed in Florence Cook then the joint sittings may at first have strengthened his belief in Mary Showers in spite of the strange reticence of Katie King when questioned about Florence Maple. But *after* Mary Showers's alleged "confession" what could he have thought if we still assume he believed in Florence Cook? Did he still really believe that a genuine Katie King would play around his laboratory with Mary Showers dressed up as Florence Maple and that then she declined to discuss the matter when asked? If, on the other hand, as Mr. Hall has suggested, Crookes was Florence's confederate . . . what motive could Crookes have had in permitting Mary Showers to give a joint sitting with Florence Cook? This would suggest that *before* he had obtained Mary's alleged confession he knew that Mary was fraudulent as well as Florence. Moreover, why did he invite Serjeant Cox to be present at this grotesque display described by the latter in the pages of *The Spiritualist*? . . . He [Cox] *must* have thought that Crookes was either a credulous fool or was himself involved in the deception. Even if Crookes, as is strongly suggested by contemporary material, was determined to achieve scientific priority in these matters and behaved in a manner severely criticized by writers who knew the facts, I do not think that this view is very helpful in coming to a decision. What is abundantly clear is that his behaviour both at the house and later suggest that something very odd indeed was going on with regard to his relations with Florence Cook. . . . All things considered, therefore, I think that Mr. Hall's suggestion as to Crookes's complicity is probably correct, and I do not think his critics have successfully disposed of it, as they seem to me to have evaded the extreme difficulties of the two unpleasant alternatives open to them, namely that Florence Cook was genuine, or that Crookes was completely deceived by her.[13]

Dingwall feels that

If, they [Medhurst and Goldney, p. 123] suggest, Crookes were convinced of Florence Cook's authenticity, then his behaviour over the Showers crisis becomes comprehensible. On the other hand, they state that as far as they know he never offered to explain away this very difficult situation of a genuine Katie King playing about with a spurious Florence Maple.[14]

4

Florence Cook's Frauds

It is time now to return to the question of Florence Cook being caught in a fraud. It will be remembered that the Volckman incident was previously discussed. This was the only notable "exposure" of Florence Cook before or during the period in which William Crookes examined her phenomena. His investigations of her were over in mid-1874. At that time, the materialization of Katie King was ended, as will be described later. Florence Cook henceforth had several new materializations, and Crookes seems to have lost interest in her.

There was one minor "exposure" of Florence Cook published in 1874, but probably describing a séance of 1872. In this case, a Mr. Hipp caught her with her hand where it shouldn't have been. The report was as follows:

> Mr. William Hipp has also recounted in the *Echo* his experience of a séance, with the celebrated Miss Cook as a medium. Among the other manifestations the time arrived for the spirits to sprinkle the guests with water, a tumbler having been placed on the table for that purpose. The room was darkened and the expectation was on tiptoe, but the sceptical Mr. Hipp grasped the tumbler, and in a few seconds clutched the hand that was dipped into it. As he had caught a spirit a light was procured, and a striking tableau presented itself. The spirit hand had an arm of flesh, which formed part of Miss Cook's body. The censure and ignominy, he adds that he brought on himself, was only counterbalanced by the satisfaction he felt in having at last caught a spirit.[1]

Florence's defense to this exposure was given by her friend Thomas Blyton,[2] who said that she had instinctively stretched her hand across the table in order to take back a flower that had been removed from her dress by spirits. Why her hand would be dipped into the water tumbler, and why she thought she could get back a flower *in the dark* and while supposedly in a trance was not explained.

Florence Cook continued to give séances and materialize forms. In 1880 Sir George Sitwell was a party in the most blatant incident involving the catching of Florence Cook in a fraud that occurred in her whole career. Sir George's son, Osbert Sitwell, has reprinted the details of this incident as "Appendix A" of his biography, *Left Hand, Right Hand.* It occurred on 2 January 1880 at a séance at which Florrie Cook was materializing "Marie," her newest spirit form. In the words of the newspaper account:

On the first visit they tied the medium with great care, and no manifestations followed. Upon the second visit, on Jan. 2, they again tied the medium, but this time under the direction of the chairman of the meeting, an official connected with the institution [the British National Association of Spiritualists]. On this occasion, either the tying was less complete, or the spirits were more accommodating, for the "spirit," which was, they were told, that of Marie, a dead child twelve years of age, came upon the scene. Certain appearances, notably the fact that the spirit wore stays, excited some suspicion in the minds of the visitors, and the next time they presented themselves at the door of the temple of Spiritualism they were accompanied by Mr. J. C. Fell, M.I.M.E., the editor of a scientific journal, and his wife. The spirit "Marie" again appeared and this time the suspicions of Sir G. R. Sitwell and his friend became excited by the sound of undressing behind the curtain where the medium sat, and the "spirit" was seized by one of the visitors, while the others, pulling aside the curtain, displayed the medium's empty chair, with her discarded dress, stockings and boots. The meeting then broke up in confusion and adjourned to a room downstairs, where all present—excepting the officials, one of whom took refuge in abuse—entirely agreed with Sir G. Sitwell and his friends, as to the grossness of the imposture, and thanked them for exposing it.[3]

While this exposure did hurt Florrie's "business," she continued to give séances until almost the time of her death in 1904.

Another minor incident which smacked of fraud occurred in 1878, when Katie King came out of the cabinet wearing a garment that some sitters recognized as belonging to Florence Cook.[4] Katie King admitted the fact of the dress's ownership, but said that it was due to the "power" not being very strong, so she had saved herself trouble by appropriating clothing belonging to the medium.

More serious was the set of séances given by Florence Cook late in her career in Warsaw, Poland. In 1899 she was declared by the committee for whom she sat to be nothing but a "miserable, badly conducted comedy" that had nothing to do with real mediumship. Mrs. Florence Cook Corner was found to have slipped her bonds, and an electrical device in her chair also had indicated that she had left that chair. (Why didn't Crookes think of using something so simple in the chairs of the mediums he investigated?) Also, Florence was wearing a white bandage on her arm, which was thought by the committee to be the source of her spirit's white robe. The committee comforted itself with the thought that Florrie must have lost her power.[5]

Another Florence Cook fraud ties in with the idea that Florrie greatly resembled her spirit, Katie King, physically. This will be discussed later. In 1873 Lord Arthur Russell wrote to *The Spiritualist* about a séance he had just attended at Hackney with Florence Cook. His account is worth quoting at length:

> I had been led by the accounts of witnesses to expect a startling apparition; it was therefore, naturally, very disappointing, after Miss Florence Cook had been tied down in the cupboard, and the ghost of "Katie" looked out of the peephole, to observe that the face was merely Miss Florence Cook's face, with a piece of white linen wrapped round it, and that the black face which subsequently appeared was again merely Miss Cook's face with black tissue drawn over it.
>
> I could not feel satisfied with the explanation of the believers present, that the spirit-faces are usually found to be strikingly like their mediums. I also thought that the alarm and indignation shown by Mrs. Cook, when I proposed suddenly to open the cupboard during the apparition of the spirit was calculated to confirm the suspicions of an unbeliever. Miss Florence Cook's often-repeated request that we should talk together while I was endeavouring to listen to the shuffling noise she made inside the cupboard, before the apparition of the face at the aperture, also produced an unfavourable impression upon me.
>
> When Miss Florence Cook was liberated, and the string with which she had been bound was cut, Lady Arthur Russell, who does not believe in ghosts, naturally picked up the string and examined it carefully. She found that the portion which passed round Miss Cook's waist, had been cut and sewn together again with white thread. The explanation suggested, that this had probably been done in the shop where the string had been bought, was, I must say, not convincing to my mind; nor was the opinion, expressed by a lady present, that the string might have been cut and mended by an evil spirit, in order to throw discredit on the phenomena of Spiritualism, at all more conclusive.
>
> During the second séance, when Miss Florence Cook had been effectually tied with pocket handkerchiefs and twine, no ghost appeared at the peep-hole. It was quite impossible for an unbeliever in spiritual manifestations, like myself, not to draw an unfavourable conclusion from

this fact when put together with the observations of the first part of the séance.[6]

We now come to Crookes's photographs of Florrie Cook and Katie King. Crookes claimed that he took forty-four such photos and that most were accidentally destroyed by Crookes himself. Although he refused to allow the photos to be publicly viewed or published, about eight have survived. These were given by Crookes to various people with the agreement that they would not be published. A number of them have now been published after Crookes's death.

The interesting thing about these photos is that while they *do* show Katie King and the form of another body in a chair or lying down, supposedly Florence Cook in a trance, *none* of the photos show the *faces* of both Florence Cook and Katie King at the same time. Katie is always either standing in front of Florrie's head blocking the view of it, or Florrie's head is covered by a cloth or something else. This is very suspicious, considering the fact that Crookes gave what he considered his best photos to people he knew who asked for them, promising that they would not publish them. If these were his *best* photos, and remember that Crookes was an *expert* photographer, why did not one photograph show both faces?

There is another interesting fact here. It can be clearly seen in some of the photos that we are dealing with *two* human beings. Assuming one of them to be Florence Cook (it is not certain *which* one), who was the other? Either it was a materialized spirit, *or* it was a confederate, but who? Florence Cook had a younger sister named Kate Salina Cook. We know Florence Cook was quite short (about 5′ 2″). Katie King was about four inches taller, according to Crookes. That would make her 5′ 6″. We know Katie King looked a good deal like Florrie Cook, but was not identical, again according to Crookes.[7] Could the part of Katie King have been played by Kate Salina Cook? Our ability to answer this question is made a great deal harder by the fact that there are no known photographs of Kate Salina Cook. Trevor Hall tried to find one, suspecting the impersonation was done by her, but was unable to find a photograph.[8] Hall tends to think that Kate Salina Cook was *not* the confederate,[9] but only because Kate Cook was often present in the audience at her sister's séances. We do not know, however, if she was present during the *entire* séance, or only at the beginning and end. No one seems to have taken notice.

Hall discusses the possible role and person who may have served as confederate for Florrie Cook as follows:

The role of the confederate who lay on the floor of the bed-room, clad in one of Florence's dresses and with a shawl over her head, would not be an onerous one. The friend, suitably dressed, would obviously be in the house before the sitters arrived, probably in the kitchen quarters, and would secretly enter the bed-room by the side door after the curtains had been drawn. She would take up Florence's position on the floor, thus leaving the medium free to play the part of the materialization. The insistence that the sitters [sang] hymns during this period would obviously cover any noise inadvertantly made. . . . The confederate may have been Caroline Corner, who at the relevant time was Florence's sister-in-law. It is noteworthy that whilst Caroline with her mother had been a constant sitter at Florence's earlier séances before the Mornington Road era, she was conspicuously absent from the Hackney sittings. Mrs. Amelia Corner attended a number of them as a member of the old Dalston group.[10]

Caroline Corner was frequently the person who "searched" Florence in the early days when no one could enter the cabinet. Such a confederate doing the searching would not be likely to mention the clothes that Florence was concealing to dress the materialization of Katie King. Another possible confederate is Mary Rosina Showers, who we know was a fake medium and who often worked with Florence Cook. Hall thinks Showers is the most likely confederate.[11]

Finally, Crookes reported that he had cut off a lock of Katie's hair and also a square of cloth from her dress.[12] The dress supposedly repaired itself instantly, with the hole closing up and disappearing. Crookes told Lord Robert Lytton that he (Crookes) still had the cloth and hair in 1891. Lord Lytton quite logically pointed out in his letter of that year to Mrs. Earle that

If the spirit [the materialization of Katie King] were a phenomenon produced by the temporary combination of certain forces or molecules, it appears to me that no separate feature of it could permanently survive its otherwise total cessation. . . . But here the lock of hair and the pieces of the dress, years after the spirit has totally and finally disappeared, remain unchanged and apparantly subject to all the ordinary laws and conditions of ordinary matter, they being, nevertheless, integral parts of the apparition, and the apparition itself fleeting phenomena.[13]

Quite so.

Let us summarize what we know or can be fairly confident about Florence Cook and her phenomena[14]:

- "Katie King" and Florence Cook bore a striking enough resemblance to each other that it is likely that Florence impersonated Katie.

- All the facts about Florence and her family lead us to the conclusion that she was fraudulent.

- The only evidence that we have that Florence Cook possessed paranormal powers is Crookes's word for it.

- Crookes had free access to the medium's cabinet in séances held in his own home, and perhaps elsewhere, so he must have known that Florence and Katie King were the same person.

- The conditions under which the séances were held were designed to make fraud possible.

These reasons appear to me to make a strong case for the fraudulence of Florence Cook. Yet, we must remember, Crookes pronounced her genuine. What Crookes's motivation for doing so may have been will be discussed in Part Two.

Part Two

Sir William Crookes
The Scientist

5

Biographical Sketch of Sir William Crookes

William Crookes (1832–1919) was born in London, the eldest of sixteen children of a prosperous tailor. He received irregular schooling until he enrolled in the Royal College of Chemistry in 1848. He became the student of A. W. Hofmann, the director of the school. Although Crookes was a gifted student, he was approaching chemistry from a nontraditional route, as most future top scientists went through the university. However, Crookes soon came to the attention of Michael Faraday. Faraday ecouraged Crookes to go into what was then called "chemical physics," and is today known as physical chemistry. Both Faraday and Crookes shared a brilliance at experimental method and a lack of great mathematical ability.

Charles Wheatstone obtained the position of superintendent of the meteorological department of the Radcliffe Observatory at Oxford for Crookes upon his graduation. In 1856 Crookes moved to London, where he combined a private analytical laboratory in his home with the editorship of several scientific journals, among them *Chemical News*. Crookes married Ellen Humphrey of Darlington, and eventually had ten children. His hard work and broad scientific interests went largely into supporting his large family and into trying to prove to the world that pure scientific research could lead to financial rewards.[1]

Crookes was a brilliant experimentalist, with a great deal of careful and patient observation going into his experiments. Among his discoveries were the element thallium, although there is some dispute over this,[2] and the Crookes Tube. This was the predecessor of the cathode-ray tube that is found at the heart of television sets, and was responsible for the first production of X-rays and the discovery of the electron, although Crookes himself just missed discovering either of these himself. Crookes also invented two devices that have minor utility: the spinthariscope, which registers

51

radioactive decay as flashes on a phosphor screen, and the radiometer, which demonstrates the force of radiant energy. By the 1870s Crookes was speculating about theoretical scientific matters, and served as a synthesist of other scientists' ideas and hints.

In 1867 Crookes's brother Philip died at sea. William was quite close to Philip, and the possibility of contacting him "in the spirit world" was a real motivation to try to apply the rigorous methods of the laboratory to spiritualist manifestations. Although Crookes's fellow scientists warned him that he would be ridiculed for investigating spiritualism, Crookes persisted for nearly five years. It was the cooperation of D. D. Home as an experimental subject that enabled Crookes to begin his investigations of mediums in early 1870.

After Crookes ended his formal investigations of spiritualism in 1874, he resumed his straight scientific work. He was a member of the Society for Psychical Research from its founding in 1883. He served as president of the society from 1896 to 1899 and as president of the Royal Society from 1913 to 1915, having been made a fellow of the Royal Society in 1863. He was knighted in 1897, receiving the Order of Merit in 1910. Crookes's wife died in 1916, and he died on 4 April 1919 in London.

6

Crookes's Explanations of Spiritualism

Crookes had several theories he thought might account for the phenomena he saw. In his article in the *Quarterly Journal of Science* for January 1874, entitled "Notes of an Enquiry Into the Phenomena Called Spiritual," he outlined his ideas as follows[1]:

First Theory—The phenomena are all the result of tricks, clever mechanical arrangements, or legerdemain; the medium[s] are impostors, and the rest of the company fools. It is obvious that this theory can only account for a very small proportion of the facts observed. I am willing to admit that some so-called mediums of whom the public have heard much are arrant impostors who have taken advantage of the public demand for spiritualistic excitement to fill their purses with easily earned guineas; whilst others who have no pecuniary motive for imposture are tempted to cheat, it would seem, solely by a desire for notoriety. I have met with several cases of imposture, some very ingenious, others so palpable, that no person who has witnessed the genuine [!] phenomena could be taken in by them. An enquirer into the subject finding one of these cases at his first initiation is disgusted with what he detects at once to be an imposture; and he not unnaturally gives vent to his feelings, privately or in print, by a sweeping denunciation of the whole genus "medium." Again, with a thoroughly genuine medium [!], the first phenomena which are observed are generally slight movements of the table, and faint taps under the medium's hands or feet. These are quite easy to be imitated by the medium, or by anyone at the table. If, as sometimes occurs, nothing else takes place, the sceptical observer goes away with the firm impression that his superior acuteness detected cheating on the part of the medium, who was consequently afraid to proceed with any more tricks in *his* presence. He, too, writes to the newspapers exposing the whole imposture, and probably indulges in moral sentiments about the sad spectacle of persons, apparently intelligent, being taken in by imposture which he detected at once.

There is a wide difference between the tricks of a professional conjurer, surrounded by his apparatus, and aided by any number of concealed assistants and confederates, deceiving the senses by clever sleight of hand on his own platform, and the phenomena occurring in the presence of Mr. Home, which take place in the light, in a private room that almost up to the commencement of the *séance* has been occupied as a living-room, and surrounded by private friends of my own, who not only will not countenance the slightest deception, but who are watching narrowly every thing that takes place. Moreover, Mr. Home has frequently been searched before and after the *séances,* and he *always* offers to allow it. During the most remarkable occurrences I have occasionally held both his hands, and placed my feet on his feet. On no single occasion have I proposed a modification of arrangements for the purpose of rendering trickery less possible which he has not at once assented to, and frequently he has himself drawn attention to tests which might be tried.

I speak chiefly of Mr. Home, as he is so much more powerful than most of the other mediums I have experimented with. But with all I have taken such precautions as place trickery out of the list of possible explanations [!].

Be it remembered that an explanation to be of any value must satisfy *all* the conditions of the problem. It is not enough for a person, who has perhaps seen only a few of the inferior phenomena, to say, "I suspect it was all cheating," or, "I saw how some of the tricks could be done."[2]

It is at this point that Crookes begins his "Second Theory," but I will take leave of him for a minute to comment upon what he has just said. It is obvious at several points in his explanation that Crookes has already made up his mind that there are "genuine" mediums. He can think that, but it should not be a part of his possible theorizing, except as a separate entry. Crookes's thinking is hopelessly naive if he really thinks that magicians can only produce their illusions when at their own places and surrounded by all of their large equipment. Many fine illusions require virtually no equipment, and can be performed almost anywhere. It is an extraordinarily uncautious observer, especially one claiming to be a scientist, who will virtually rule out trickery as even a possibility, as Crookes has done.

Crookes's "Second Theory" is as follows: "The persons at a *séance* are the victims of a sort of mania or delusion, and imagine phenomena to occur which have no real objective existence." Although Crookes makes no comments at this point about his second theory, it is obvious that he holds no brief for it.

Crookes's remaining theories are as follows:

Third Theory—The whole is the result of conscious or unconscious cerebral action. These [last] two theories are evidently incapable of embracing more than a small portion of the phenomena, and they are improbable explanations for even those. They may be dismissed very briefly. I now approach the "Spiritual" theories. It must be remembered that the word "spirits" is used in a very vague sense by the generality of people.

Fourth Theory—The result of the spirit of the medium, perhaps in association with the spirits of some or all of the people present.

Fifth Theory—The actions of evil spirits or devils, personifying who or what they please, in order to undermine Christianity and ruin men's souls.

Sixth Theory—The actions of a separate order of beings, living on this earth, but invisible and immaterial to us. Able, however, occasionally to manifest their presence. Known in almost all countries and ages as demons (not necessarily bad), gnomes, fairies, kobolds, elves, goblins, Puck, etc.

Seventh Theory—The actions of departed human beings—the spiritual theory *par excellence.*

Eighth Theory—(*The Psychic Force Theory*)—This is a necessary adjunct to the 4th, 5th, 6th, and 7th, theories rather than a theory by itself. According to this theory the "medium," or the circle of people associated together as a whole, is supposed to possess a force, power, influence, virtue, or gift, by means of which intelligent beings are enabled to produce the phenomena observed. What these intelligent beings are, is a subject for other theories.

It is obvious that a "medium" possesses a *something* which is not possessed by an ordinary being. Give this *something* a name. Call it "x" if you like. Mr. Serjeant Cox calls it Psychic Force. There has been so much misunderstanding on this subject that I think it best to give the following explanation in Mr. Serjeant Cox's own words:

> The Theory of *Psychic Force* is in itself merely the recognition of the now almost undisputed [!] fact that under certain conditions, as yet but perfectly ascertained, and within a limited, but as yet undefined, distance from the bodies of certain persons having a special nerve organization, a Force operates by which, without muscular contact or connection, action at a distance is caused, and visible motions and audible sounds are produced in solid substances. As the presence of such an organization is necessary to the phenomenon, it is reasonably concluded that the Force does, in some manner as yet unknown, proceed from that organization. . . . This is the force to which the name of *Psychic Force* has been given by me as properly designating a force which I thus contend to be traced back to the Soul or Mind of the Man as its source. . . . The difference between the advocates of

Psychic Force and the Spiritualists consists in this—that we contend that there is as yet insufficient proof of any other directing agent than the Intelligence of the Medium, and no proof whatever of the agency of Spirits of the Dead; while the Spiritualists hold it as a faith, not demanding further proof, that the Spirits of the Dead are the sole agents in the production of all the phenomena.[3]

What we have here is a real puzzle. If Cox is correct, then the phenomena are genuine in many cases, but produced by the medium. If that is so, then the *content* of the phenomena, namely messages purporting to come from departed spirits, are *not* genuine, since they do not come from spirits but rather from the medium. Are the phenomena themselves, filled with erroneous contents, *still* genuine? If so, what does the word "genuine" mean?

7

Crookes's Motivation

In his book-length biography of Crookes, Edward Fournier d'Albe states that there are two possible ways of viewing Crookes's involvement with spiritualism. His involvement occupied the years 1869 to 1874, with active public involvement from 1870 to 1874. Fournier d'Albe calls the two viewpoints "the Rationalist version" and "the Spiritualist version." As the way he defines these so clearly delineate the major problem historians have had with Crookes, it is best to simply reproduce what he says:

Spiritualist Version—Crookes was an eminent man of science inclined to agnosticism. He was an insatiable investigator, ever ready to probe into new and unknown phenomena. Modern spiritualism, born in America in 1848, presented to the world an ever-increasing array of baffling phenomena having within them a spiritual meaning and a message to humanity. Crookes was not primarily interested in the message, but was keenly interested in the physical phenomena, and anxious to bring them under the reign of natural law. He had a very happy manner with mediums, being courteous and gentlemanly without the least relaxation of scientific vigilance. This somewhat rare combination of qualities accounts for his marvellous and unprecedented success. His experiments with D. D. Home were classical and absolutely free from flaw. They were sufficiently rigid to stand the keenest scientific scrutiny. Their rejection by the Royal Society is but another sad illustration of the blindness to new facts sometimes shown by conservative corporate bodies. In any case, the facts convinced Crookes personally of the reality of psychic phenomena. His further experiments with Florence Cook convinced him that there was a super-mundane intelligence behind the phenomenon, and so he finally became a convinced spiritualist. His great task being accomplished, he returned to his laboratory work and gave to the world the

Crookes tube and the radiometer. But he remained a spiritualist for the rest of his life.[1]

Crookes's termination of his research on spiritualism would be explained by the spiritualist version as follows:

> Let us try to put ourselves into Crookes's mental attitude on both hypotheses. On the spiritualist version he would have gone through a profound spiritual crisis on the death of his brother. He would feel defeated by the powers of darkness. Being a man of great power and resource, he would rebel against the powers of darkness, and would look about for means of defying and defeating them in turn. His victory over death would be assured if he could throw a bridge across the chasm. He had heard that such bridges had been thrown already. Why, then, should he not construct a better bridge, built on scientific principles, a bridge of permanent use to mankind, the greatest feat of bridge-building ever attempted! Having set to work on this great attempt, he proceeded as he always did in his investigations, collecting and sifting raw material, following every promising track, recovering himself then temporarily lost, and following steadily the beckoning light ahead. The light would no doubt in the end grow into a blaze, and would perhaps reveal the glories of hidden worlds to come!
>
> In the end, having had a glimpse of those glories such as has been given to few mortals, but having entirely failed to exhibit them to his colleagues, and having been overwhelmed with aspersions and ridicule from the public, and quarrels with old friends, he would close the chapter and return to his older avocations, with the pure light of another world shining forever on his inmost soul. Such a state of mind would be quite consistent with what we know of Crookes's character and dominant impulses.[2]

Fournier d'Albe defines the rationalist version as follows:

> *Rationalist Version*—Crookes, like many another physicist, had a streak of mysticism in his mental constitution. The death of his brother under tragic circumstances threw him into spiritualism. Being, like most scientific men, rather guileless himself, he fell an easy victim to the imposters who were then ministering to what had become a society craze in England. D. D. Home succeeded in gaining his entire confidence and then in duping him by his trickery. Being already a convinced spiritualist, Crookes was incapable of applying scientific tests to any matter involving his rather vivid personal feelings. In any case, he was by his training absolutely unfitted to detect the clever methods of fraud which had been evolved by mediums since 1848. So he was deceived both by Home and Florence Cook. He probably in the end suspected that all was not well, and in

1874, he decided to have done with the matter for ever. Having publicly committed himself to raps, levitations, and "materialisations," he did not like to retract. But he abruptly closed a rather unfortunate chapter in his career, and made amends by an unparalleled devotion to pure science, which soon brought forth abundant and refreshing fruit.[3]

Crookes's termination of his research would be explained via the rationalist version as follows:

How are we, then, to figure to ourselves the mind of the same man on the "rationalistic" hypothesis? We must assume a predisposition in favor of the supernatural, intensified by a grave personal bereavement. Meeting others who had passed through similar crises, and had found consolation in spiritualism, he would try the same path, and, in order to succeed, would throw himself into that passive and devotional attitude alleged to be favorable to the development of spirit manifestations. He would begin, perhaps, in his intimate family circle, and observe table movements and planchette writings under conditions when deliberate deception, even in a family of mischievous young children, would apppear as a monstrous absurdity. Having thus obtained a *prima facie* conviction that "there was something in it," he would go further, and gradually come into touch with the more advanced exponents of the new cult. He would by then consider himself capable of telling the true from the false, and would go chiefly to those mediums who inspired him with confidence. On his finding such a medium, there would be no limit to his trustfulness, and he would be his [or her] convinced and active champion. He would throw himself wholeheartedly into the conflict of opinion then raging, and would try to secure fresh evidence to support his point of view. He would be, as ever, a "bonnie fighter," and be willing to give and take hard knocks. But in the end he would find out his mistake of placing any confidence in the professional medium. He would sicken of the perpetual useless struggle, and would at length realise that science and spiritualism were incompatible and incommensurable, science being of the mind and spiritualism being of the heart. He would return to his first allegiance, and keep his private longings out of sight. He would still give all mediums the benefit of the doubt, and would not retract anything he had said. But he would "pull up short," and refuse to advance further into the swamp.[4]

Although I don't think that I could have stated the two positions better, obviously both could not be true. In fact, *neither* is likely to be the entire explanation. Perhaps *elements* of each contain the truth when properly combined. Although at this late date we cannot know the whole truth, perhaps we can use what evidence is available to us to approximate Crookes's motivation in his spiritualistic investigations.

The charge has been made by a number of people, including Trevor Hall,[5] that William Crookes's methods of investigating Florence Cook were much sloppier and less scientific than those he employed in testing Daniel Home. John Palfreman says this was not so.

> The truth of the matter was that Crookes was also having sittings with Herne, Williams and Kate Fox at the same time he was investigating D. D. Home. The nature of these sittings was far more akin to the Florence Cook séances than the D. D. Home experiments. The fragmentary records of such investigations indicate that on April 12, 1871—a very early date in Crookes's "Spiritualist" career—he was apparently witnessing some very extreme phenomena.[6]

One of Crookes's motivations, after he had begun to examine spiritualism, was his belief that he had discovered a new, fourth state of matter in the universe—"radiant matter"—with solid, liquid, and gas as the other three. In this Crookes was somewhat mistaken, although *part* of what he was thinking was correct. He was working on what was to become the radiometer at about this time. The radiometer is a little set of "weather vanes" that can rotate in a glass bulb that contains a partial vacuum. It was thought that the force that causes the vanes to rotate when light shines on them was due to what is now called "radiant energy." This was an unknown force at the time. In fact, Crookes, in effect, discovered the existence of radiant energy, although he was mistaken about its composition. He thought it was made up of molecules, whereas we now know it is made of photons of light. Although radiant energy was *not* the same "force" that the mediums, and especially D. D. Home, used, as Crookes thought, Crookes was at least aware that some unknown mechanism was active in the movement of the radiometer vanes. It turns out that Crookes's explanation of what made the vanes turn when light was shined on them was wrong. The movement turns out to be due to the fact that the black side of the vanes absorbs more heat energy from the light than the white side of the vanes. It then radiates this energy, which strikes the remaining air molecules in the bulb, producing the force that turns the vanes.

Sir William Barrett, who gave the memorial address at the Society for Psychical Research after Crookes's death, said of him that

> One would have thought Sir William Crookes would have been the most unlikely man of science to take up the investigation of psychical phenomena. His hands at the time were full of pressing scientific and literary work; moreover, his somewhat austere temperament and his passion for exact data and extreme accuracy in all his experimental researches naturally sug-

gest that he would look with scorn on the contradictory, loose and inconclusive psychical evidence which existed when he began his investigations.[7]

We can now examine some of the contradictions in Crookes's behavior, before we finally see what he was really trying to do. First, it should be noted that Crookes, in spite of his pretensions to objectivity, was a *convinced* spiritualist in 1870—*before* he began his investigations of D. D. Home or Florence Cook. This can be seen from an extract from his private diary, dated 31 December 1870, that is reprinted in *Crookes and the Spirit World* (pp. 234–35). Crookes asks God to "allow us to continue to receive spiritual communications from my brother who passed over the boundary [into the spirit world] when in a ship at sea more than three years ago." He also says, "and when the earthly years have ended may we continue to spend still happier ones in spirit land, glimpses of which I am occasionally getting."

At the same time, Crookes wrote to Madame Boydanof of St. Petersburg, Russia, on 1 August 1874 that

> During this whole time [i.e., 1869–74] I have most earnestly desired to get the one proof you seek—the proof that the dead can return and communicate. I have never once had satisfactory proof that this is the case. I have had hundreds of communications *professing* to come from deceased friends, but whenever I try to get proof that they are really the individuals they profess to be, they break down. Not one has been able to answer the necessary questions to prove identity; and the great problem of the future is to me as impenetrable a mystery as it ever was. All I am satisfied of is that there exist invisible intelligent beings, who *profess* to be spirits of deceased people, but the proofs which I require I have never yet had; although I am willing to admit that many of my friends declare that they have actually received the desired proofs, and I myself have been very close to conviction several times.[8]

How can we reconcile these two apparently contradictory positions? It is not difficult if we accept the statement of C. C. Massey, an original member of the Society for Psychical Research Council, who states in a letter written to Col. R. S. Olcott, a prominent theosophist, that he (Massey) had had a long conversation with Crookes at dinner (December 1875) in which Crookes had revealed that he was an occultist and a follower of Eliphas Levi.[9] These people believe in spirits, but feel that they are independent beings —like angels, perhaps—and *not* the remains of dead humans. That is, the spirits exist, but they do not have the same personalities as living humans. This position, if indeed Crookes held it, would square the two apparently contradictory positions above. In fact, we do know that Crookes joined the Theosophists in 1883, and remained a member for the rest of his life.[10]

Crookes gives two instances of phenomena he witnessed in séances (one with Home),[11] which, *as described,* are inexplicable except by the interaction of spirit entities. These will serve us as good examples of the types of problems that exist with regard to published reports.

When sitting with Mr. Home, a wood lathe (stick) was lying on the table. It moved over to Crookes's position and began tapping him on the hand. Home's hands were visible on the table top, not touching the lathe. Crookes asked out loud if the lathe could tap out a message in Morse code, knowing that he was the only one there who knew Morse code, and *he* did not know it well. The stick immediately began tapping out Morse code so rapidly that Crookes himself was only able to catch a word or two of the message.

A second instance of the inexplicable occurred while a medium (unnamed) was using a Ouija board. Crookes asked out loud if the "intelligence" directing the movement of the medium's hands on the Ouija board could "see" the contents of the séance room. The answer was yes. Crookes then reached behind him to a table upon which was a copy of the *London Times*. He placed his finger on the newspaper without looking, and asked if the "intelligence" could indicate via the Ouija board what word his finger was covering. The word "however" was spelled out. When Crookes turned around to see what word his finger was covering, he saw that it *was* "however." The medium could not have seen the newspaper print or the covered word from where she was sitting.

Another puzzling incident involving Crookes occurred in a séance held at Hackney on 29 March 1874.[12] Crookes reported that he went into the medium's cabinet, walking behind Katie King. There he found Florrie Cook, apparently lying on the floor. With the use of a phosphorous lamp, Crookes inspected Florrie, ascertaining that it was she by shining the light on her face. While he held one of Florrie's hands in his, he shined his light upon the standing form of Katie King. She did not speak, but moved her head and smiled. All the while Florrie appeared to be in a trance. As Florrie awakened, Katie motioned to Crookes to leave. Katie then disappeared. From the above, we can see that either Crookes was thoroughly fooled by Florrie Cook (it is hardly likely that he could not recognize that either Katie or Florrie was being portrayed by a confederate), *or* that Katie and Florrie really were a medium and her materialized spirit (unlikely, since most of the other evidence in this book is against that interpretation), *or* that Crookes was in on the deception as an active participant (strange, but my reluctant conclusion).

Crookes had forty-four photographs of Katie King and/or Florence Cook, taken during séances. Some he calls "excellent."[13] Yet *none* of these, to the best of anyone's knowledge since many have been destroyed, has ever surfaced that showed the *faces* of both Katie King and Florrie Cook *in the same photograph.* Crookes says that he has only one photograph of the two together, "but Katie is seated in front of Miss Cook's head." Crookes's failure to produce just *one* photograph of the two together showing both of their faces (which would have gone far toward substantiating his case that Florrie and Katie were not both just Florrie) is *inexplicable* unless Crookes was in on the deception, which would mean that he *could not* have had a photograph showing both of their faces simultaneously. *That* would have shown that most of the time Florrie was being "played" in trance by a confederate or by a bundle of her clothes.

Crookes states that "it was a common thing for the seven or eight of us in the laboratory to see Miss Cook and Katie at the same time, under the full blaze of the electric light."[14] If so, why did none of the "seven or eight" ever testify in print to having seen this? Also, just two lines above this quote, it is stated that "Katie muffled her medium's head up in a shawl to prevent the light falling upon her face." If that light was dangerous, as claimed, when the "seven or eight" saw them both "in the full blaze of the electric light," the face of the medium was still muffled in a shawl. How did the viewers know who was under the shawl? This contradiction about having seen both Katie King and Florence Cook together makes no sense unless Crookes is being deceptive.

As Dingwall points out in his *Critics' Dilemma,*

It is true that Mr. Benjamin Coleman, one of the most enthusiastic of the group of Spiritualists in the 1870s and who claimed Crookes as his "excellent pupil," tried in 1874 to get the said pupil to answer a few straight questions about Katie King. To Coleman's surprise, Crookes refused to answer his letter and never mentioned the matter to him again. This "studied reticence," as Coleman called it, seemed to him very odd, as odd indeed as the whole set-up at the Cooks' home at Hackney seemed to another of the old stalwarts, Samuel Carter Hall, who was once present at a séance where, if fraudulent, a confederate seemed likely, but if so then, he thought, the whole family must have been involved, including Crookes himself. To Mr. S. C. Hall, this seemed unlikely, although he gave it as his opinion that he could imagine Crookes to be a rogue rather than a fool, an ally rather than a victim.

The dilemma facing Mr. S. C. Hall was precisely that of modern writers. Can it really be believed that Crookes, who actually acted as Florence Cook's manager and controller of many sittings, was so blindly credulous that *if* she were fraudulent *he* was deceived? *If* again she were fraudulent and Crookes was not deceived, he *must* have been the rogue and ally mentioned by S. C. Hall. On the other hand, Florence, of course, *may* have been genuine and Katie King a real "materialization." If this be so, then Crookes's way of recording this astounding miracle, his extraordinary behaviour at the sittings—described by one observer as half-showman and half play-actor—and his studied reticence when questioned by the man who claimed him as his pupil becomes, to me at least, inexplicable.[15]

We now come to the "smoking gun" in the case against Crookes. It occurs in a passage in a letter from Serjeant Edward Cox to *The Spiritualist* of 26 March 1875. Many others have probably read this letter, and have not seen the implications clearly. However, reading it again, the implications struck me. Cox was a thoroughly honest and rational man whose skepticism has been apparent in a number of quotations I have given from him. He would not allow himself to believe in anything that did not make perfect logical sense to him. The materializations did not. Cox says that when testing Annie Eva Fay with the Varley electrical apparatus, he saw that while Mrs. Fay was supposedly attached to the apparatus and while it was *not* indicating any release of the handles that the medium was supposed to be holding, that the entity handing books and other objects through the curtain (only the arm could be seen) was Mrs. Fay herself. Cox claimed that he could see through a crack in the curtain that

It was the perfect form of Mrs. Fay—the hair, the face, the blue silk dress, the arms bare below the elbow, and the pearl armlets! At that moment the instrument [galvanometer] gave no sign of any break of contact with the wires her hands were grasping, and the form appeared on the side of the curtain opposite to that where she had been seated, and distant at least eight feet from her chair, so that if it were taken down by herself she must have parted from the wires [the apparatus] for the purpose. Yet did they betray no sign of broken contact.[16]

The implications of this are staggering. No confederate could have been used under these circumstances since the confederate would not have appeared identical to Mrs. Fay. No materialized spirit could have been responsible, as the materialization would again not have been identical to Mrs. Fay. Mrs. Fay, in addition, was later to admit that she was a fake. She even tried to go on a tour, showing how she did her tricks. Either Mrs. Fay, on her own and with a team of electrical experts, broke into Crookes's lab, hooked herself up to the equipment to figure out how much resistance her body had when measured on this apparatus, and then managed to produce a resistance of that value to place in the circuit, *or* Crookes himself measured her body's resistance, gave her a resistor of the proper amount, and instructed her about how to substitute the resistance into the circuit. This would all have had to be done before the first Varley test that was given to Mrs. Fay. We know from experiments made in the 1960s by Brookes-Smith that similar equipment to that used had about a four-second "lag time" before it responded to a "disconnection."[17] That would only be known to Crookes. The possibility remains that a confederate grasped the handles of the Varley device within four seconds after Mrs. Fay released them. However, that person needed to have a body resistance nearly identical with that of Mrs. Fay. The confederate would have had to been tested and smuggled into the cabinet in Crookes's own house. There appears to have been no way in which this could have been done without Crookes's knowledge and compliance.

There are additional complications here. First, the resistance of the human body varies greatly, even when measured through the same points. Figures of from 10,000 to 500,000 ohms are considered legitimate. The variation depends upon (1) the type of electrode paste/contact made with the skin, (2) the amount of sweating done by the subject, (3) the body temperature of the subject, (4) the relative humidity in the room, and (5) the emotional state of the subject (this is the basis of the polygraph's use of the galvanic skin response to detect lies).

We also have the problem of an inadequate description of exactly how Mrs. Fay (or Florrie Cook) was brought into contact with the hand-held electrodes in most of the experiments. Was either of the mediums actually observed while taking hold of the "handles"? Was an initial resistance measurement made at that time, while the medium was actually observed holding the electrodes? The alternative is that the medium was simply allowed to go behind the curtain in the cabinet and *told* to grasp the electrodes. If *this* was the case, slipping *any* resistance into the circuit *at that point* which was in the range of say 50,000 to 200,000 ohms would have fooled the Varley device and defeated its purposes. The small possibility that *this* incredibly sloppy experimental procedure could have been used is the only method that allows Mrs. Fay to have cheated without the requirement that William Crookes was a party to the deception. However, Mrs. Fay is not likely to have had enough knowledge of electrical circuits in the 1870s to have come into the experimental setting with a resistor in the proper range of human bodily resistance. She would have needed Crookes's or some other scientist's help. That shifts suspicion back to Crookes. He could also be accused of stupidity in experimental design, but that is not likely to have been the case.

If Mrs. Fay was made to hold the handles and a first reading taken while she was under observation (one would hope that the experiment had been designed in this way by Crookes), we are left with no other reasonable alternative but that Crookes was an active planner in the deception that Mrs. Fay was going to perform before a group of Crookes's scientific colleagues.

When we consider what Crookes's motive could have been in doing this, we must remember one other rather startling fact, namely that Mrs. Fay's Varley test occurred about a year *after* Florence Cook was hooked up to the same equipment by Crookes.[18] Florence's test had been about 1 March 1874. By the time Mrs. Fay was tested, Florence was no longer producing the materialization of Katie King (her last appearance was on 21 May 1874).[19] Therefore, Crookes could not have had any motivation regarding Florence Cook when he decided to fake Mrs. Fay's Varley test. We must look for some other reason why Crookes would *continue* to deceive his fellow scientists, as he had in the case of Florence Cook.

First, in fairness, it must be pointed out that Cox changed his story slightly after four years. He tried to explain what he had seen by presenting as fact something he did not mention in his first letter to *The Spiritualist*. Four years later, according to Medhurst and Goldney,[20] he says that he *also* saw behind the curtain "another form, like we had left upon the seat, grasping the handles [of the apparatus], still there, still in the same posture, but too much in shadow to enable me to note the dress." We must take this with several grains of salt. First, the source of this quotation is not given by Medhurst and Goldney, who are usually meticulous in their documentation. Second, this detail appears to have been added by Cox in order to enable him to rationally explain what he thought was happening. Third, it is doubtful that he could see what was happening eight feet behind the curtain in a darkened room through a small crack in the curtain, especially with the medium's body blocking the line of view through the crack in the curtain. Finally, the presence of a *fake* body of Mrs. Fay holding the handles of the equipment makes no sense if the *real* Mrs. Fay was extending her arm through the curtain, since no one could see the chair where the medium was supposedly sitting. Cox's explanation of four years later, although accounting for all of the facts, is highly dubious. He said that the medium's body, in trance, was standing behind the curtain. The medium's "spirit form" was sitting in her chair. This involves a concept—"spirit form"—whose existence remains to be demonstrated, and it reverses the usual spiritualist explanation that the medium's entranced body remains in the chair, while her materialization moves to another location in the room. Cox is trying to make a rational explanation for what he saw, realizing that the only alternative explanation to his is to accuse Crookes of fraud and deception.

Crookes's own account of one of the four electrical tests of Annie Eva Fay was published in *The Spiritualist* of 12 March 1875, and is reproduced in Medhurst and Goldney. One paragraph is worth reprinting here, as it tells of Crookes's thoughts about how the Varley apparatus could be cheated. Using a damp handkerchief, Crookes reports that

> By a series of careful adjustments, between each of which they had to ask me what amount of deflection had thus been produced upon the galvanometer outside, they in time obtained an amount of resistance the same as that of a human body, but to effect this would have been impossible without information as to the indications given by the galvanometer outside, and all this time the violent oscillations of the ray of light showed that they were trying to make a new contact by tricks of some kind.[21]

Of course, Crookes may be using a red herring here in order to divert attention from the fact that a premeasured resistor *could* have been custom-made to cheat the device in another way entirely. It should be remembered that the "smoking gun" electrical test was done on 19 February 1875, so it was not *this* séance. The resistor would have been made prior to *that* test, if indeed one had been made. Yet, Crookes wrote a letter within nine weeks after this test (the 12 March test) to R. Cooper of Boston, Massachusetts, in which he says,

> In reply to your favor of October 25th, which I have received this morning, I beg to state that *no one* has any authority from me to state that I have any doubts of Mrs. Fay's mediumship. The published accounts of the test séances which took place at my house are the best evidence which I can give of my belief in Mrs. Fay's powers. I should be sorry to find that any such rumors as you mention should injure Mrs. Fay, whom I always found most ready to submit to any conditions I thought to propose.[22]

To return to Crookes's motivation, I can think of only one such reason, although there may be others. Crookes was a convinced spiritualist, and he wanted to dignify spiritualism with a scientific imprimatur: A scientist had investigated spiritualism and had pronounced it genuine. It boggles the mind to think that Crookes was so imbued with this desire that he would spend several years faking his results in order to deceive his fellow scientists and the public, but it is the only conclusion that seems to make sense given the facts that we have.

Finally, here are a few thoughts to put in perspective the "smoking gun" and the motivation of Crookes in the previous Florence Cook investigation. As Dingwall points out in his *Critics' Dilemma,*

> It is interesting that when it was a question of the mediumship of D. D. Home there was apparently no hesitation [on the part of the Society for Psychical Research] in asking both Sir William and Lady Crookes

for their comments on the certain sittings (see *Proceedings*, SPR, 1894, IX, pp. 308, 310). There must have been some reason why Crookes maintained this attitude of secrecy about Florence Cook to the end of his life and why those who had the opportunity did not question him on certain puzzling aspects of the case, such as the connection between Miss Cook and Miss Showers and the famous letter from Lady Crookes on the Leila materialization.[23]

Also, as Ian Stevenson pointed out in his rather negative review of Trevor Hall's work on Crookes and Cook,

It would seem that Crookes permitted conditions in the séances with Florence Cook to be considerably more lax than they had been in his earlier investigation of D. D. Home, and we have no satisfactory explanation of this. Perhaps her attractiveness for him had led him to neglect the canons of control which he himself had enunciated earlier. We remain puzzled also by Crookes's failure to circulate the photographs he took of Katie King (in which some discern an impressive resemblance of facial features between Florence and Katie); by his failure to report and comment on Varley's galvanometer experiments; and by his failure to name and provide corroborating testimony from other witnesses present at the séances he supervised or attended.[24]

Perhaps the last needed perspective on the whole Crooks/Cook investigation should be that of Serjeant Edward Cox, author of the "smoking gun" letter. As quoted by Dingwall, Cox summarizes his doubts about Florence Cook's and Mary Rosina Showers's materializations as follows.

All the prescribed conditions are such as facilitate trickery, if designed, and to prevent, and not promote inquiry . . .
. . . This unquestionable likeness of the form to the medium. When I saw them they were not merely resemblances; they were facsimilies . . .
. . . But the difficulties do not end there. Assuming the forms to be Mesdames Morgan [Katie King] and Maples (whom they claim to be), who lived on earth some years ago, and who ever since have been dwelling in spirit land, how comes it that they think the thoughts and speak the languages and have the manners of girls of the year 1874, instead of the very different ideas, structure of talk and manners of (their) own time? And, more than this, why does Miss Maples play upon the piano tunes that have been composed since her death, and sing songs of recent date, instead of those that were known to her in life?[25]

Just so.

Sir William Crookes, circa 1872. Author's collection.

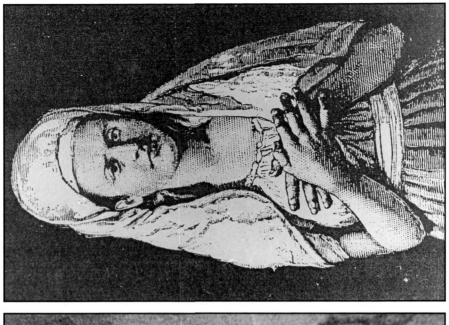

Left: Florence Cook, circa 1875. Courtesy Harry Price Library, University of London. **Right:** Drawing of the "materialization" of Katie King. Author's collection.

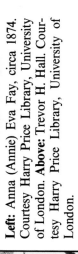

Left: Anna (Annie) Eva Fay, circa 1874. Courtesy Harry Price Library, University of London. **Above:** Trevor H. Hall. Courtesy Harry Price Library, University of London.

Daniel Dunglas Home. Courtesy New York Public Library.

Left: One of D. D. Home's accordions. Author's photo of instrument at the Society for Psychical Research, London.

Bottom: D. D. Home and accordion in Crookes's cage. Author's collection.

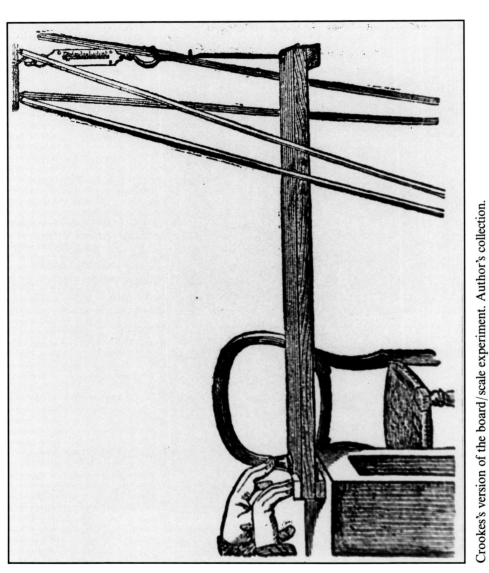

Crookes's version of the board/scale experiment. Author's collection.

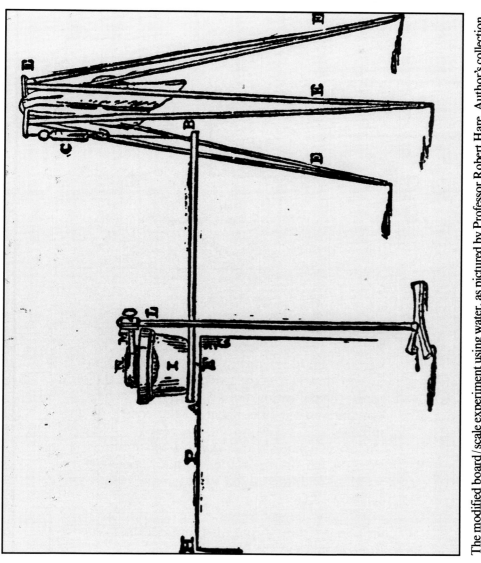

The modified board/scale experiment using water, as pictured by Professor Robert Hare. Author's collection.

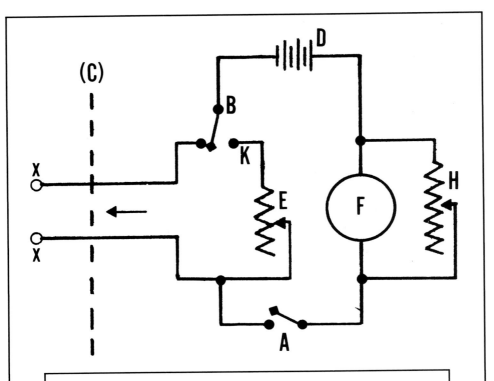

The Varley Apparatus

D   Battery, about 6 volts.

F   Reflecting galvanometer.

H   Variable shunt resistor to bypass most of the current flow across the galvanometer and thus adjust the deflection.

E   Variable resistor to duplicate the resistance of the subject.

A   On/off switch (shown in the "off" position).

B   Press-switch, shown in the "normal" operating position (with the subject's body in the circuit across X–X).

C   Position of the wall between the laboratory and the library ("dark" room where subject was located).

X–X   Brass handles in the library, to be held by the subject.

The Varley Apparatus. Courtesy James Randi.

Part Three

Daniel Dunglas Home
The Medium

8

Biographical Sketch of D. D. Home

Daniel Dunglas Home (1833–1886) was one of the best known physical mediums of the nineteenth century. His life remains a puzzle, despite several full-length biographies.[1] It remained for Trevor Hall to show that Home's middle name, Dunglas, which represents one of the noble Scottish families, was really just an affectation.[2] In other words, Home, although he often claimed the descent of his father as a "natural [i.e., illegitimate] son of Alexander, tenth Earl of Home," was actually not related to that family, and therefore not a Dunglas. In addition, his birth certificate does not have Dunglas on it; it's simply Daniel Home.[3] In fact, the presence of the name Dunglas was a powerful tool to curry favor and acceptance among the aristocrats with whom Home associated for much of his life.

In reality, Daniel Home was born at Currie, near Edinburgh, Scotland, on 20 March 1833. He was the son of William Home and Elizabeth McNeill. Daniel was adopted when he was a year old by his childless aunt, Mary Cook. He lived with her at Portobello, on the coast of the Firth of Forth in Scotland, until he was nine years old. At that time, his aunt's family moved to the United States, settling at Norwich, Connecticut. There Daniel stayed until he was twenty-two. At that time, his aunt supposedly threw him out of the house following a long series of what we today call "poltergeist incidents," centering about Daniel. Daniel had become a successful medium, following the craze for spiritualist phenomena that followed upon the Fox sisters' popularizing of spirit knocking ("raps"), beginning in 1848. By 1851 there were reportedly over one hundred mediums in New York State alone.[4] By 1855, when Home was twenty-two years old, the mediumistic craze had started to fade in the United States. Home had friends who offered to pay his fare to England, and a convinced spiritualist who owned a hotel in London offered to board him for no charge. Home left for England on 31 March 1855, arriving in England in April of that year.

Home had arrived in England at precisely the right time, as there was a great deal of interest in spiritualism, yet few really good mediums. Home's reputation spread rapidly and soon he was in great demand. From the beginning he refused direct payment for his services, insisting instead that lodging, food, or a gift (especially of jewelry) would be welcome. In return for this, Home required that he have the final say about who could attend his séances. It was a brilliant move, as it allowed Home to keep out rival mediums, arch skeptics, magicians who might see through the methods used, and others who might disrupt or prove hostile.

Home was also a master at understanding the use of publicity. He managed to get Lord Brougham and Sir David Brewster, a well-known scientist, to attend one of his séances. When Brewster was at first impressed by the phenomena, and then later said that he had seen nothing unusual, Home accused him of lying, although not by name. There was much publicity, but Brewster refused to be further drawn into the controversy.

Home spent much of the time between 1855 and 1862 in London and in Italy, France, and Russia. He gave séances at the homes of the wealthy and of European royalty. Again, he never charged for his sittings, but accepted room and board and gifts. When royalty was involved, these gifts were often expensive jewelry. During his travels in Russia, Home met his future wife, Alexandra, the daughter of a highly placed general named de Kroll. The Czar Alexander II himself gave his blessing to the marriage, which occurred in Russia in August 1858.

After Home's first wife died in 1862, her estates were seized by her relatives in Russia. None of the money and assets Home thought he had inherited were available to him. Instead, there was a lengthy court battle over the estates. In the meantime, Home went to Rome, where he tried to earn a living as a sculptor. He also published the first volume of his *Incidents in My Life* (1863), supposedly largely written by his solicitor, W. M. Wilkinson. Home was expelled from Rome by the papal government in 1864, on the grounds that he was a "sorcerer."

In 1866 Home's financial troubles were eased somewhat by his friend Samuel Carter Hall, who founded the "Spiritual Athenaeum," a society in London that provided a position for Home as its resident secretary, as well as a place for him to live. The arrangement led Home to perhaps the most disastrous incident in his career, namely his involvement with Jane Lyon.

Lyon was a wealthy widow, evidently not too bright or educated, who approached Home in his capacity as secretary of the Spiritual Athenaeum in an effort to get in contact with her deceased husband by spiritualist means. Home conducted a séance for her on 3 October 1866. She was "successful" in contacting her husband Charles's spirit. Home was rewarded with a check for fifty pounds. Other séances followed. Mrs. Lyon claimed that Home gave her directions from her late husband that Home was to be treated like a son. He was to have the sum of twenty-four thousand pounds (the equivalent of $100,000 then, and probably more like $1 million in purchasing power now) made payable to him. This was done two days later when Home took Mrs. Lyon to her stockbrokers to complete the transaction. Home arranged to have his solicitor friend W. M. Wilkinson draw up a new will for Mrs. Lyon. The will left all her property to Home exclusively. A later séance in December 1866 brought the instructions from her late husband to give Home a birthday present of six thousand pounds.[5]

In February 1867, with Mr. Wilkinson's help, a further thirty thousand pounds was given to Home. Several months later, Mrs. Lyon had second thoughts about the whole procedure, and instituted suit to get the money back. It is not clearly known whether this was, as has been reported, because she went to another medium (reportedly Mrs. Nichols, later known as Mrs. Guppy)[6] who told her that Home was a fraud, or because, as has also been suggested, she did not find that Home gave her the access to royalty that she had hoped would impress her relatives.[7]

In any case, the suit was filed in Chancery Court, and was decided on 1 May 1868.[8] The judge ruled that Home had used improper influence upon Mrs. Lyon, namely spiritualistic messages purportedly from her dead husband, to get Mrs. Lyon to sign the money over to him. The judge ordered Home to return all sixty thousand pounds to Mrs. Lyon. Home complied, but how he could afford to do so is not clear, as some of the money had been sent to the United States to help purchase a new home for his aunt. Perhaps some of Home's rich friends helped.

Public opinion was not highly favorable to Home after this case. It was given great publicity, and at the end Home found his career was at an all-time low. However, while the case was being heard, Home was already cultivating the friendship of Lord Adare, whom he had first met in November 1867. This friendship was to lead to the publication of a book about Home's phenomena that was so startling that it revived his career.

Viscount Adare, heir to the wealthy Irish Adare family, was Home's constant companion from late 1867 to early 1869. At that time, Adare became engaged to the woman he was later to marry, and the pending marriage indicated to Home that his close relationship with Adare would be ending. During that two-year period, Home often stayed with Adare at one of the family's London pied-a-terres, namely Ashley House in Ashley

Place. It was here, on the evening of 16 December 1868, that Home's famous levitation out one window and into one in the next room occurred. This is discussed in detail in a later chapter, "The D. D. Home Levitations." The point that concerns us here is that Home's ability to maintain his lodging with Adare was about to end. His career was at a low ebb in the public's mind because of the Lyon case. Home needed to do something to restore his reputation quickly. The speed-up of the publication of Adare's book *Experiences in Spiritualism With Mr. D. D. Home* was done. It was published by Adare's father, the Third Earl of Dunraven, largely from letters written to the father by the son, detailing his experiences at Home's séances. The book appeared in July 1869, as Trevor Hall has shown,[9] and only fifty to seventy copies were printed privately. It became even rarer since soon after publication and distribution of copies to friends of the Adares, the author/publisher approached all who had been given copies and asked that they be returned. Most were returned and then destroyed. Hall goes into the probable reason for their recall,[10] which he speculates was pressure from the Roman Catholic church upon the Earl of Dunraven, a recent Catholic convert. However, several published reviews of the book, and possibly copies reaching the wealthy friends of Adare, had the intended effect. Home's popularity was largely restored.

The investigation of Home's mediumship by William Crookes, whom Home contacted via Professor Aksakoff in late 1869, also helped. Crookes pronounced Home genuine in 1871, and they remained friends and correspondents for many years. In October 1871 Home married for the second time. His wife was Julie de Goumeline, a member of the wealthy Russian Aksakoff family. *This* wife had actual access to her wealth, and it enabled Home to retire from his spiritualist work.

The timing was most fortunate for Home. In 1871 the newest craze in mediumship, namely full-form materialization, was just beginning. Mrs. Guppy actually started it, but Florence Cook, Mary Rosina Showers, and others brought it to full development. There was a great danger for Home in these materializations, however, and he probably realized it. All it took was one overzealous attendee at a séance who grabbed the materialized spirit, and any fakery was instantly revealed. It was a dangerous game to play, as Florrie Cook's several exposures in exactly this way were to show. Home decided that it was time to retire, at least from active mediumship. He moved to France with his new wife. His health was declining. Home worked for a while on the second volume of his *Incidents in My Life* (1872), and on his history of spiritualism, *Lights and Shadows of Spiritualism* (1877). The latter book is notable mostly for the fact that it contains a chapter revealing the tricks used by fraudulent mediums. It would seem, according to Home, that virtually every medium other than himself was fraudulent.

After the publication of *Lights and Shadows of Spiritualism,* many of his fellow mediums probably changed their opinion of Home. Of course, the book made him look better. The book also reveals several other things about Home's own feelings about spiritualism. For example, there is a long section in the book in which Home makes it clear that he feels the idea of spirits being involved in the return of personalities to the earth in the form of reincarnation is incorrect.[11] Home strongly opposed Allan Kardec's ideas about reincarnation. (Kardec was a French spiritualist who was the founder of one of the important schools of spiritualism and one that exists to this day, especially in Brazil.) Home's 1877 book also contains one of the very few comments that he made in print specifically about Crookes's tests of Florence Cook. It is worth quoting: "Concerning genuine materializations, I need hardly remind my readers that the carefully-conducted experiences of Mr. Crookes with Miss Cook were repaid by evidence giving undeniable certainty to the phenomenon."[12] Also interesting is Home's repeated insistence, mentioned here again, that "I have never yet beheld anything which could cause me to accept the asserted phenomenon of matter passing through matter."[13]

Home's wife Julie adored him, frequently having to nurse him through some difficult health crises. Home, it would appear, had tuberculosis, although it is difficult for us to know for certain exactly what his ailment was. His first wife Alexandra ("Sacha") apparently died from TB after a four-year marriage. This may or may not be a clue to Home's own illness, but it certainly is suggestive.

Daniel Dunglas Home eventually died in June 1886. He was buried in the cemetery at St. Germain-en-Laye, France. After his death, his wife completed two biographical volumes, largely from letters and magazine articles. They were *D. D. Home: His Life and Mission* (1888) and *The Gift of D. D. Home* (1890).

The two books by Mrs. Home consist largely of the texts of letters attesting to Home's great powers by recounting actual incidents to which the letter writers were eyewitnesses. Some of the letters describe quite amazing things. One of the first suspicions of some investigators upon the publication of *D. D. Home: His Life and Mission* was that the letters had not been faithfully transcribed or were not authentic. F. W. H. Meyers, working for the Society for Psychical Research, made a trip to France in 1889 to meet with Mrs. Home and to examine the actual letters. He compared them with the published text. Meyers attests that the letters are authentic and have been quoted correctly.[14] I also examined the letters, now in the Cambridge University Library, in 1990, and agree with Meyers's conclusions.

However, something should be stated here with regard to Home's other books, i.e., those that he is supposed to have written himself. Meyers and Barrett reproduce a statement from W. M. Wilkinson, Mr. Home's solicitor, that *he* (Wilkinson) actually wrote *Incidents In My Life* for Home.[15] Wilkinson is also given credit for having been the real author of Home's *Lights and Shadows of Spiritualism* (1877) and possibly of the Second Series of *Incidents In My Life* (1872). This information is mentioned not to impeach Home, but rather to indicate that the incidents in the volumes written by Wilkinson and by Mrs. Home are now no longer firsthand evidence, but secondhand, having filtered through their minds. There is the additional problem that Mrs. Home wrote her biographies in French, and they were then translated into English by Home's former secretary, John Veitch.[16]

9

Home's Phenomena

There are a number of phenomena attributed to D. D. Home that have not been discussed before. His levitations are the subject of a separate chapter. In this chapter will be discussed his bodily elongation, "spirit hands," fire resistance, the movement of objects without being touched, raps, and accordion playing with one hand.

Bodily Elongation

There were many eyewitnesses to Home's elongations. Supposedly, he could add eleven or twelve inches to his height. One testimony about a Home elongation (written in 1868, shortly after the event occurred) was by H. D. Jencken, a convinced spiritualist. He says that

> Lord —— [Adare] was seated next Mr. Home [sic] who had passed into a trance state, in which after uttering a most beautiful and solemn prayer, he alluded to the protecting spirits whose mission is to act as guardian angels to men. "The one who is to protect you," he said, addressing Lord —— [Adare], "is as tall as this." And upon so saying, Mr. Home grew taller and taller; as I stood next to him (my height is 6 feet) I hardly reached up to his shoulder, and in the glass opposite he appeared a full head taller than myself. The extension appeared to take place from the waist, and the clothing separated 8 to 10 inches. Walking to and fro, Mr. Home specially called our attention to the fact of his feet being firmly planted on the ground. He then grew shorter and shorter until he only reached my shoulder, his waistcoat overlapping to the hip.[1]

There are several other accounts by Jencken, Lord Adare, and others of Home's elongations. In fact, Home himself said in 1868 "Daniel has been elongated six times, he will be elongated thirty times during his life."[2] Yet there is nothing inexplicable about Home's elongations.

Elongations have been an occasional feature of vaudeville and side-show acts for many years.[3] Perhaps the foremost of these "elongators" was Clarence E. Willard, who performed his act in vaudeville around 1910, and continued for twenty years. Willard was known as "The Man Who Grows." He was normally 5' 9" tall, but could add eight inches to his height and possibly more. As magic historian Christopher has noted, Willard kept his feet firmly planted on the stage, but, when he was finished elongating, his vest was far above his trouser tops. His chin was also higher than the tallest person in the audience. Willard could also stretch his arms until they appeared to grow by more than twelve inches.

This elongation was *not* a fake, as Willard was tested under medical observation. Although to a small extent the elongation was aided by an optical illusion, Willard had actually learned how to stretch his body and limbs. Willard explained his technique to a meeting of the Society of American Magicians in 1958. He claimed that his constant stretching in previous years (he was retired before 1958) had actually added two inches to his normal height. Ricky Jay also mentions Willard and a number of other professional elongators.[4]

An additional Home elongation was described by the Master of Lindsay, although he does not give the date or location.

> On another occasion I saw Mr. Home, in a trance, elongated eleven inches. I measured him standing up against the wall, and marked the place; not being satisfied with that, I put him in the middle of the room and placed a candle in front of him, so as to throw a shadow on the wall, which I also marked. When he awoke I measured him again in his natural size, both directly and by the shadow, and the results were equal. I can swear that he was not off the ground or standing on tiptoe, as I had full view of his feet, and, moreover, a gentleman present had one of his feet placed over Home's insteps, one hand on his shoulder, and the other on his side where the false ribs come near the hip-bone.[5]

Lord Lindsay added the following to his testimony in response to questions from the Dialectical Society:

> The top of the hip-bone and the short ribs separate. In Home they were unusually close together. There was no separation of the vertebrae of the spine; nor were the elongations at all like those resulting from expanding the chest with air; the shoulders did not move. Home looked as if he

was pulled up by the neck; the muscles seemed in a state of tension. He stood firmly upright in the middle of the room, and before the elongation commenced I placed my foot on his instep. I will swear he never moved his heels from the ground. When Home was elongated against the wall, Lord Adare placed his foot on Home's instep, and I marked the place on the wall. I once saw him elongated horizontally on the ground; Lord Adare was present. Home seemed to grow at both ends, and pushed myself and Adare away.

The elongation still seems to fit the Willard method, especially where the tense muscles are noted.[6]

Spirit Hands

There were a number of sittings by D. D. Home, mostly in the early part of his career, when "spirit hands" appeared. These were usually glowing hands that appeared around the séance table and touched various people seated at that table. Among the reasons why the sitters thought that these hands were "spirit hands" and not the hands of Home or a confederate were the following: (1) Home's hands were visible on the top of the table and were *not* being held by anyone, (2) the spirit hands often ended at the wrist where nothing further could be seen, and (3) the hands often seemed to melt away if they were grasped by people. It must be remembered that the lights were turned down at this part of the séance.

In Crookes's summary of "Hand Phenomena," which he included in his article in the *Quarterly Journal of Science,* it is noted that hands were "frequently felt at dark séances, or under circumstances at which they cannot be seen." At another time,

a small hand and arm, like a baby's, appeared playing about a lady who was sitting next to me. It then passed to me and patted my arm and pulled my coat several times. . . . Sometimes, indeed, they [the spirit hands] present more the appearance of a nebulous cloud partly condensed into the form of a hand. . . . At the wrist, or arm, it becomes hazy, and fades off into a luminous cloud. To the touch, the hand sometimes appears icy cold and dead, at other times, warm and life-like, grasping my own with the firm pressure of an old friend.[7]

Crookes's observations, as far as they went, were accurate here. His interpretation of what he had seen was not. Crookes has failed to examine what fraudulent methods could have been used to produce the effects that he saw. Rather than suspect a trick, he accepted what he had seen as being *genuine,* and then had been unable to explain what he saw in those terms. Yet Crookes has provided us with the clues that will help us solve the spirit-hands mystery.

Daniel Home was an excellent sculptor. He even tried to make a living as a professional sculptor in Rome for a short period, and at Florence as well. One of his special skills was sculpting hands. There are reports that his studio in Italy was filled with sculpted hands.[8] It is quite notable also that Home's own hands have been described as very long and thin, and quite distinctive. Consider this possibility, and it is only a possibility because no one seems to have thought of it before or explored it when it could have been investigated: Since no one was controlling Home's hands at most of his séances, but rather it was noted that both of his hands were visible on the table in the dim light, was it possible that Home simply substituted one of his sculptured hands (perhaps of lifelike wax), with an attached sleeve, for one of his own hands on the table? That would allow him to have one of his hands free when needed. It should be noted that Home was almost never searched before or after a séance. He was a guest in the home, after all, and it would be rude to treat him like a suspect. With one hand free, Home could do a great many things that could not be done otherwise.

We must also note the charge that has been made that Home used his feet to produce many of the tappings and spirit-hand phenomena. Mr. F. Merrifield, for example, saw Home with some sort of hand attached to his own arms at a séance.[9] This incident will be further discussed in the chapter on "Charges of Fraud Against Home." Nevertheless, this is a piece of evidence that Home used sculpted hands (in this case on the end of an extension or "reaching rod") to do some of his spirit-hand effects.

The glowing or light-emitting hand, often seen by Crookes and others, can be explained by means of the use of "oil of phosphorus." This interesting substance, made by dissolving a piece of white phosphorous in a vial of olive oil for several months, is something we know Home experimented with. One of the charges of fraud against Home (see chapter 11) involved the discovery that he was doing something with a vial of oil of phosphorus, was caught, and abandoned the vial on a mantelpiece. At any rate, oil of phosphorus produces a white light when it is exposed to the air. An object smeared with the oil and kept in an oxygen-free atmosphere will glow when exposed to oxygen or air. Another source of glowing light was an object coated with calcium (or zinc) sulphide and then exposed to a strong light for a while. This object (or the coating on it, to be more precise) will emit light for a short period in the dark, then will slowly fade out. This fading out is precisely the behavior noted for some of the spirit hands. Perhaps it is the multitude of methods by which the spirit hands could be produced that has caused people to hesitate to explain how they were made. The fact that when the hands were grasped they sometimes felt cold (these were sculpted models) and sometimes felt warm (these were probably Home's foot) is explained by the several methods used. The fact that a number of people who held the hands found that they "melted away" when grasped posed a mystery to me for a while. That a reference was found to the fact that the end of a foot, when grasped by a hand, can slip out of the grasp and feel exactly as if it were melting away solved this mystery.[10]

Fire Resistance

D. D. Home, at one point of his career, did several séances in which he demonstrated his resistance to heat and flame. Most of these incidents involved Home's picking up, handling, or stirring up hot coals from a fireplace. Several of these demonstrations were witnessed by William Crookes, who describes one such incident as follows:

> Mr. Home again went to the fire, and after stirring the hot coal about with his hand, took out a red-hot piece nearly as big as an orange, and putting it on his right hand, covered it over with his left hand, so as to almost completely enclose it, and then blew into the small furnace thus extemporised until the lump of coal was nearly white-hot, and then drew my attention to the lambent flame which was flickering over the coal and licking round his fingers; he fell on his knees, looked up in a reverent manner, held up the coal in front, and said, "Is not God good? Are not his laws wonderful?"[11]

Crookes described another of Home's experiments with fire in a letter to Mrs. Honywood on 28 April 1871. This letter can also be found in the *Proceedings of the Society for Psychical Research,* as follows:

> At Mr. Home's request, whilst he was entranced, I went with him to the fireplace in the back drawing-room. He said, "We want you to notice particularly what Dan is doing." Accordingly I stood close to the fire and stooped down to it, when he put his hands in. He very deliberately pulled lumps of hot coal off, one at a time, with his right hand, and touched one which was bright red. He then said, "The power is not strong on Dan's hand, as we have been influencing the handkerchief most. It is more difficult to influence an inanimate body like that than living flesh, so, as the circumstances were favorable, we thought we would show you that we could prevent a red-hot coal from burning a hand-

kerchief. We will collect more power on the handkerchief and repeat it before you. Now!"

Mr. Home then waved the handkerchief about in the air two or three times, held it above his head, and then folded it up and laid it on his hand like a cushion; putting his other hand into the fire, he took out a large lump of cinder red-hot at the lower part, and placed the red part on the handkerchief. Under ordinary circumstances it would have been in a blaze. In about half a minute he took it off the handkerchief with his hand, saying "As the power is not strong, if we leave the coal longer it will burn." He then put it on his hand and brought it to the table in the front room, where all but myself had remained seated.[12]

The above "performance" is in no way unique to D. D. Home. Many magicians, even today, incorporate a "fire resistance" trick into their repertoire. In fact, the above is one of the clearest instances of Home's straight magic performances.

There is nothing inexplicable about the incident. In fact, the trick can be performed by a number of different methods, most of which involve switching the borrowed handkerchief for a different, fire-resistant one. Home was wary of performing too much straight magic, lest magicians rush to denounce him, and he never seems to have publicly repeated this trick.

Locating a Magnet in the Dark

Lord Lindsay reported that he hid a large magnet in a dark room. He then asked Home if he would be willing to try to find it in the dark. Home agreed to do so. When brought into the room,

He then said that he saw some light on the floor in a corner of the room, and immediately said to me—"Give me your hand and I will show you exactly where I see it." He then led me straight across the room and without the least hesitation stooped down and placed my hand on the magnet.[13]

There is a ready explanation for Home's ability to locate the magnet. It is an effect known as "muscle reading" and done by a number of mentalists even today. Recall that Home took Lindsay *by the hand and led him* to the magnet. A skilled muscle reader can tell by the tension in your arm and hand with each step that he leads you, exactly whether he is going in the correct or incorrect direction.[14] When you are going in the wrong direction, the muscles tense up in the arm of the person who knows where the object is hidden. Yes, it takes skill and practice, but it does not involve anything inexplicable or unknown. Another possibility is the use of a luminous compass needle, which Home could use to lead him to the magnet.

The Self-Playing Accordion

There are several reports of an accordion, what we would today call a concertina, being played while being held by only one hand on the non-key side.[15] There are also reports of the accordion being played while no one was holding it at all.[16] This instrument consisted of a small bellows with a wooden square containing a handle on each end. On one end were some leverlike keys. The instrument (see photo insert) was played by holding one handle in each hand, fingering the keys, and simultaneously stretching and compressing the central bellows by moving the hands closer together and further apart. It would appear to require two hands to play the instrument, one of which had to be on the end containing the keys.

Home supposedly could cause the accordion to play while hanging it vertically, with only one hand on the non-key side. Crookes tested Home's ability to do this by providing a wire cage into which one of Home's hands, holding the accordion vertically by the non-key side, was placed. Although Home's other hand could not be introduced into this cage, the accordion was still heard to play.

The explanation for this phenomenon eluded me until James Randi told me[17] that William Lindsay Gresham, who was writing a book about Home that unfortunately was not completed before his death (nor ever published), had discovered a small harmonica among Home's effects held at the Society for Psychical Research in London. This harmonica, containing one octave, could be concealed in the mouth. It should be recalled that Home wore a bushy mustache, further aiding the concealment of the harmonica. The tone of a harmonica is very similar to that of a small concertina. Although the concertina that Home used was still in the society's offices as of 1990, the harmonica has vanished. Assuming that Gresham was correct—and we have no reason to suspect that he was lying—the sound of the accordion was produced by Home playing the concealed harmonica. In the dark, with the concealment by his mustache, in combination with the expectation of hearing an accordion, the simple one-octave tune that was produced (usually "Home, Sweet Home") would appear to have come from the accordion. The movement of the bellows of the instrument that was occasionally reported is easy enough to produce if you can "catch" the lower end of the instrument upon some hook or protrusion. Then simple wrist action can produce the movement of the bellows. The weight of the lower handle alone may be sufficient.

Table Tipping

There are several ways that table tipping or the levitation of furniture (usually tables) can be accomplished. One method requires a confederate, and it would appear that Home rarely, if ever, used one. To levitate a table with a confederate, a device that is strapped to the wrist under the shirt is often used. This device has a flat blade, similar to that of a chisel, that extends to the middle of the wearer's hand. With both hands flat on the top of the table, the blade is slipped under the table's top ledge. This requires an accomplice to do the same thing on the opposite side of the table if levitation is to occur. With only one user of the device, table tipping only can be achieved. The wearer of the device slowly rises from his or her seat at the table, claiming that the table is rising and forcing him or her to rise with it. The illusion is even better if each person's hand is touching the hand of the person next to him or her. The rising table then appears to be "dragging" each person up with it. If only one person is using the device, then merely pushing away with it, at a slightly upward angle, will cause the table to tip.

This report of Hamilton Aïde provides a remarkably clear example of the probable use of a table-lifting device of this sort by Home.

> The table becoming more and more obstreperous, Home said, "I think it will ascend. We had better all rise from our seats, but *keep our hands upon the table.*" [emphasis in the original] On hearing this, Alphonse Karr claimed his right to break the circle, and go down upon all-fours, which accordingly he did. We rose, pushing our chairs back, and standing as far away as possible, consistently with keeping our hands upon the table, which then began slowly to ascend. It did so to a sufficient height to enable Karr to get under it, after he had grovelled round, examining everybody's feet. The length of time that the table remained in mid-air was, I should say, from two to three minutes, though it probably was not as long as that at its extreme altitude—between three and four feet from the ground. It was high enough for all of us to see Karr, and to see also that no one's legs moved: while our hands never shifted, the fingers being pressed downwards upon the table. Then, after Karr's investigation was well over, it began equally slowly to descend.[18]

There is a device described by Gresham[19] that can be used by only one person to cause even the heaviest table to tip. This is a hinged steel bar, covered with black velvet. It can be concealed under the jacket, then slipped under the center post of a heavy séance table. The bar has a "stirrup" on the end closest to the medium. By stepping on the stirrup, the table can be "levered up," causing it to tilt. The advantage of this device is that it works with even the heaviest Victorian tables used for séances.

Dingwall states that Home's phenomena were of four major types, namely, (1) raps and movements of furniture, (2) levitation of furniture and of Home himself, (3) spirit hands, and (4) communication with spirit entities.[20] Already discussed have been spirit hands and raps or movement of furniture; levitations will be discussed in a separate chapter. That leaves only "communication with spirit entities."

Home was not a major proponent of communication with spirits. It would seem that he did it mostly because his audience *wanted* to get into contact with their supposed spirit loved ones. In fact, at one point Home actually says that he believes that spirits are not the surviving personalities of specific dead people.[21]

Incidentally, Dingwall mentions that Henrietta Ada Ward, the wife of the painter Edward Matthew Ward, said in her memoirs that a lady used to help Home during the séances she attended and "act as a medium."[22] To my knowledge, this is the only place that an assistant to Home has ever been mentioned. We will keep this in mind when the possible use of confederates is discussed later.

10

The D. D. Home Levitations

It is little known, even among people quite aware of his famous levitation out one window and into another in December 1868, that Home practiced or gave a dress rehearsal for the feat on 20 November 1868. On that date, H. D. Jencken reported,

> Mr. Home had placed himself at the window, which he opened, and deliberately stepped upon the ledge outside, looking on to the street, some 80 feet below, with utter unconcern. The Honorable the ———— [Master of Lindsay] said he shuddered, alarmed at what he was witnessing. Mr. Home noticing this stepped down and reproached his friend, saying "Little faith, little faith; Daniel will not be injured." Home also had a spirit, talking through him, discuss how Home might be lifted into the air. He was to be lifted first on to the back of Lord Adare's chair. Adare felt his feet there, then he appeared to be lifted up and carried to the other side of the room.[1]

This was done in complete darkness, and probably served to prepare the minds of the sitters for the main event, coming up on Sunday, 13 December.

At Adare's rooms in Ashley Place, London, the levitation of 13 December was described as follows. It should be kept in mind that the various accounts of what happened contradict each other on a number of points. This is Lord Adare's account:

> Home then got up and walked about the room. He was both elongated and raised in the air. He spoke in a whisper, as though the spirits were arranging something. He then said to us, "Do not be afraid and on no account leave your places"; and he then went out into the passage. Lindsay suddenly said, "Oh, good heavens! I know what he is going to do; it

is too fearful." ADARE: "What is it?" LINDSAY: "I cannot tell you, it is too horrible! Adah [the spirit of actress Adah Isaacs Menken] says that I must tell you; he is going out of the window in the other room, and coming in at this window." We heard Home go into the next room, heard the window thrown up, and presently Home appeared standing upright outside our window; he opened the window and walked in quite coolly. "Ah," he said, "you were good this time," referring to our having sat still and not wished [sic] to prevent him. He sat down and laughed. CHARLIE [Wynne]: "What are you laughing at?" HOME: "We are thinking that if a policeman had been passing, and had looked up and seen a man turning round and round along the wall in the air he would have been much astonished. Adare, shut the window in the next room." I got up, shut the window, and in coming back remarked that the window was not raised a foot, and that I could not think how he had managed to squeeze through. He arose and said "Come and see." I went with him; he told me to open the window as it was before, I did so; he told me to stand a little distance off; he went through the open space, head first, quite rapidly, his body being nearly horizontal and apparently rigid. He came in again, feet foremost, and we returned to the other room. It was so dark I could not see clearly how he was supported outside. He did not appear to grasp, or rest upon, the balustrade, but rather to be swung out and in. Outside each window is a small balcony or ledge, 19 inches deep, bounded by stone balustrades, 18 inches high. The balustrades of the two windows are 7 feet 4 inches apart, measuring from the nearest points. A string-course [narrow ledge], 4 inches wide, runs between the windows at the level of the bottom of the balustrade; and another 3 inches wide at the level of the top. Between the window at which Home went out, and that at which he came in, the wall recedes 6 inches. The rooms are on the third floor.[2]

Trevor Hall has stated that there are a number of contradictions in the testimonies of the three witnesses to Home's levitation (Lord Adare, Captain Wynne, and the Master of Lindsay).[3] There is some discrepancy over the date, the location, the brightness of the moon, the height of the windows from the ground, and worse, perhaps, the actual events themselves. Hall has established that the levitation actually occurred on 13 December 1868 at Ashley House, Ashley Place, London, and *not* on 16 December at Buckingham Gate (Earl Dunraven's London address), or Victoria Street. Although the figure "85 feet above the street" has been given by Frank Podmore[4] (and he may have gotten it from Jencken's article), Hall had the height of the windows estimated by an architect from a photograph of the Ashley House building. It had been demolished by the time Hall became interested in it. The estimated height was

32 feet 6 inches above the ground. He had the architect estimate the distance between the windows as 4 feet 2 inches apart (not 7 feet 4 inches).

However, Archie Jarman, a friend of Hall, seems to have actually measured the building itself in 1964, while it was still standing. The building was demolished about 1970. Jarman's article was published in 1980[5] and seems to have been unknown to Hall. Jarman says that the windows were 7 feet 4 inches apart, as Adare had said. He also measured the distance from the bottom of the windows to the ground as 45 feet. Jarman tried to cross the space between the two balconies by means of the string-course, but found this impossible because of the fact that his center of gravity was thrust too far out from the wall, making a fall inevitable. Yet, Jarman discovered that there were steel bolts protruding from the building on either side of the balconies. These had been intended as fasteners for what were called "perambulator blinds," a kind of fan-shaped shutter that shaded the plants on the small balconies. It was possible, Jarman thought, for a heavy cord to have been fastened by Home to the two bolts at the near ends of the balconies. With this cord securely attached, it could serve as a support at the back of a man as he edged his way along the string-course. In other words, Home could easily have passed from one balcony to the other with the aid of a rope that would be unobservable except if someone had leaned out of the windows. This is one possible explanation of what happened.

Another suggestion has been made by Alice Johnson that Home actually opened the window in the other room and then sneaked back in the darkness to the first room, where he stepped up on the window sill *inside* the window.[6] He then opened the window in back of himself by turning his hands backwards. Once the window was open, he simply stepped into the room from the window sill. It is very difficult, Johnson claimed, to see in the dark if a person is standing inside or outside of a given window. We must remember at this point that actual almanac checking has shown that it was two days after the new moon on 13 December, so there was only a tiny sliver of moon to illuminate the scene, contrary to what Adare claimed. In addition, a new moon sets soon after sunset, further decreasing the amount of outside light available. Of course, Johnson's explanation does not account for the fact that Home was later seen, according to Adare, entering and exiting the window in the other room in a horizontal position.

Trevor Hall's explanation requires that the balconies be closer together than they apparently were. Hall thinks that they were close enough together so that Home, who was unafraid of heights, could simply have stepped from one to the other. However, if Jarman's measurements are correct, this could not have been done. Why Hall chose to ignore the measurements of a man whom he claims was his friend is difficult to understand. Of course, Jarman's measurements render Hall's explanation untenable, but they still do allow Home's levitation to be explained in purely natural terms.

Home was involved with other levitations besides the famous one at Ashley House. His first recorded levitation occurred at the house of Ward Cheney in South Manchester, Connecticut, in 1852, before Home left America. The evidence that Home had levitated consisted entirely of his word that he had, plus the fact that his boots could be felt suspended in the air.[7] A dishonest medium can easily produce such an effect in a darkened room merely by removing his boots, holding them up in the air (perhaps first standing barefoot on a chair), and allowing people to feel the boots off the ground as he holds them by the tops. The standing on a chair provides the medium with a high location from which to project his voice. It also allows him to use a piece of chalk or crayon on a telescoping rod to mark the ceiling as later "proof" that he had floated up to it.

"J. G. C." records an 1866 Home levitation as follows:

> Mr. Home remarked, "I feel as if I am going to rise." The room was quite dark. He said "I am getting up," and as I was only a few feet from him, I put out my hand to him. I indubitably felt the soles of both his boots, some three feet above the level of the floor. On my doing so he said, "Don't touch me, or I shall come down." Of course, I instantly desisted, but down he came.[8]

Crookes himself recorded two Home levitations he had witnessed. The first was on 30 July 1871. Crookes says

> Mr. Home walked to the open space in the room between Mr. I.'s chair and the sideboard, and stood there quite upright and quiet. He then said, "I'm rising, I'm rising," when we all saw him rise from the ground slowly to a height of about six inches, remain there for about ten seconds, then slowly descend. From my position, I could not see his feet, but I distinctly saw his head, projected against the opposite wall, rise up, and Mr. Walter Crookes [William's brother], who was sitting near where Mr. Home was, said that his feet were in the air. There was no stool or other thing near which could have aided him. Moreover, it was a continuous glide upwards.[9]

Without Walter Crookes's comments, this whole incident could easily be explained as simply another "elongation" by Home (see chapter 9, "Home's Phenomena"). After all, William Crookes did not see Home's feet, which *could* have remained on the ground. With Walter Crookes's comments, it is difficult to know what to make of Home's levitation in this case, except that it again took place in very subdued light. That makes Walter Crookes's observation that he could see Home's feet in the air (six inches from the floor) somewhat suspect.

11

D. D. Home and William Crookes

In July 1869 D. D. Home arrived again in London, just back from Russia, with a letter of introduction to William Crookes from Professor A. Boutlerow of the chemistry department at St. Petersburg University.[1] This served to bring Crookes and Home together for the first time. Crookes's brother Philip had died of yellow fever in 1869 while aboard a ship. This greatly moved Crookes, as he was quite close to this brother. Philip's death first sparked William's interest in the possibility of contacting the dead. Hence, Home's offering of himself for experimentation by Crookes was too strong an offer for the scientist to refuse.

Home and Crookes maintained a long-term friendship. Letters were exchanged between the two for many years after the experiments were conducted. Crookes trusted Home, and Home was apparently agreeable to almost any conditions Crookes wanted to impose. At least, that's what Crookes *felt*. Home, nevertheless, was a subtle yet persuasive personality, often getting his own way without letting a person realize it. For Crookes to have trusted Home, as any modern investigator of psychical phenomena can tell you, was a *big* mistake. The proper attitude of a scientific investigator, especially when dealing with *human* phenomena, is *skepticism*. Nature doesn't try to fool scientists in the laboratory; human beings occasionally *do*. This trust of Home by Crookes may or may not have been misplaced. The point, however, is that it was counterproductive to have it placed at all.

William Crookes began his investigations of D. D. Home's mediumship late in 1869. Although Crookes reported the results of his experiments with Home in several papers, these papers were rejected by the Royal Society and were subsequently published by Crookes in his own magazine, the *Quarterly Journal of Science*. As K. M. Goldney says in her introduction to the reprint of Crookes's articles on Home, "Crookes's reports of his experiments are frequently inadequate by today's standards. He was a vain, egocentric man and took it for granted that his word was sufficient to command acceptance of what he reported."[2]

It would appear that Crookes tried to impose some sort of order or control upon Home's phenomena. He said that Home agreed to all the conditions that he (Crookes) wanted to impose, yet when we look at all the phenomena that Crookes claimed he witnessed at Home's séances, much of it is of a sort that could not easily be controlled, and it wasn't. How does one control "spirit" hands that touch people sitting around the séance table? How does one control a levitation or rapping on furniture, or objects moving without being obviously touched? Although it may be difficult to regulate these things, if they are *not* controlled, then the medium is free to utilize any method, including conjuring and fraud, that he or she wishes to use to produce the phenomena. One *cannot* call any such uncontrolled experiments "scientific experiments." Even some of the controlled experiments were designed so loosely that it is stretching things to call them "scientific."

We must understand a couple of points about conjurors and how they succeed in pulling off their illusions. If he really was a conjuror, all Home had to do was to do nothing (i.e., produce no results) when the conditions of the test were unfavorable to him. By doing so, he could insure that changes were made that were more suitable to him. He could, in effect, ensure that the light was placed were he wanted it, that the people sat where he wanted them to sit, and that the equipment was designed and placed as he wished it to be. In effect, Home could control, to a large extent, the entire test.

Another problem with Crookes's experiments with Home is that the record or report is quite incomplete. The report often does not state the date upon which the test was done, or the amount of light used. Only those details that one man of science *may* have thought relevant (e.g., the room temperature), but not those facts that might give some clues as to how a *conjuror* accomplished his feats, are given.

Crookes was cautious, even hesitant, about investigating spiritualist phenomena (at least according to his own accounts). He knew his scientific colleagues were against "dignifying" the phenomena by investigating them scientifically. Nevertheless, Crookes went ahead, even though, as he said, spiritualism is "a subject, which, perhaps more than any other, lends itself to trickery and deception."[3] Crookes was also careful to note that he wanted to be openminded, without "preconceived notions whatever as to what can or cannot be."[4]

When Crookes decided to scientifically investigate D. D. Home, he had little previous research to go on. There *were* some experiments conducted by Professor Robert Hare at the University of Pennsylvania.[5] Crookes mentions these experiments, or at least the cage-like apparatus designed by Hare,[6] and which Crookes would modify to test Home's one-handed accordion-playing ability.

Crookes, in his first mention of the need for the investigation of possible new forces in the universe, says that such tests as a "delicately poised balance should be moved under test conditions" (i.e., with no possibility of anyone touching it), and some method of adding "foot pounds" to the force of an object at the end of a lever would be good tests.[7] Indeed, Crookes tried to do tests such as these with Home.

Interestingly, Crookes seems to be aware of the need for caution, at least in 1889, when he wrote the following:

> I am not surprised at the evidence of fraud [with spiritualist phenomena]. I have myself frequently detected fraud of various kinds, and I have always made it a rule in weighing Spiritualistic evidence to assume that fraud may have been attempted, either by seen or unseen agents. I was on my guard even in D. D. Home's case, although I am bound to say that with him I never detected any trickery or deceit whatever, nor heard any first-hand evidence of such from other persons. At the same time, I should never demand that anyone should consider Home, or any other medium, as "incapable of fraud," nor should I pin my faith upon any experiment of my own or others which fraud could explain. The evidence for the genuineness of the phenomena obtained by Home in my presence seems to me to be strengthened rather than weakened by the discussions of conjuring, and the exposures of fraud which have since taken place. The object of such discussions is to transform *vague* possibilities of illusion and deception into *definite* possibilities; so far as this has not yet been done, it has, I think, been made more clear that certain of Home's phenomena fall quite outside the category of marvels producible by sleight of hand or prepared apparatus.[8]

In the latter statement Crookes was quite wrong and exhibits a faulty knowledge of conjuring possibilities.

The actual experiments of Crookes, which he conducted with D. D. Home, involved tests of force (weight and mass), as measured by spring balances or other common laboratory apparatus. One test involved the use of a mahogany board, 36 inches long, 9½ inches wide, and 1 inch thick.[9] There was a 1½-inch-thick strip screwed onto each narrow end of the board, forming feet upon which the board could rest. The board was placed so that one end rested on a table, while the other end was supported by a spring balance, which was supported on a tripod stand.

The balance was set up so that it would register the maximum weight that had been exerted upon the spring. In its untouched starting position, the balance registered three pounds. Mr. Home placed the tips of his fingers upon the extreme end of the board, which was resting upon the table. Almost immediately the balance registered a downward pressure (one hesitates to call it weight). This pressure slowly increased to nine pounds, showing a six-pound increase from the resting state. When Crookes himself put his full body weight upon the spot where Home's fingers had been, he was only able to get the scale to register an additional two pounds, and then only by "jerking" his weight up and down. Remember that Home's and Crookes's weight had been placed right above the strip of wood that served as both the foot and the fulcrum of the board.

Crookes's experiment has been criticized by Professor G. G. Stokes of the Royal Society,[10] among others. The suggestion was made that Crookes add a bowl of water above the fulcrum of the board, and that Home place his fingers in the bowl of water. This was a modification of a procedure that Robert Hare did in one of his experiments. Crookes did this new test with Home, with 1½ inches of water in the bowl. Home merely dipped his fingers into the bowl. The scale indicated a maximum force of five thousand grains, or a little more than ten ounces. This force, less than one pound, is considerably less than the force exerted by Home without the water being present. Crookes does not seem to have commented upon this discrepancy. Surely, if Home could exert a real force on the balance, he could exert it through water as well as without water. The criticism from Stokes this time was that the placing of Home's fingers into the water would have displaced some water (true), which would then have registered as additional weight (true, except that the bowl of water was located over the fulcrum of the lever). Nevertheless, the possibility remains that some of the water could have been "sloshed" far enough off the fulcrum to have registered on the scale.[11]

Another critique of this lever experiment was given by W. B. Carpenter.[12] He points out that there was no determination made of the actual downward pressure of Home's fingers. The presence of wavelike motion on the scale's indicator shows that Home may have created rhythmical vibrations on the board, in an attempt to register weight on the scale.

The famous accordion experiment of Crookes was also modified from Robert Hare's work.[13] It has been mentioned elsewhere in this book that Home could easily have produced the sound of the accordion (concertina) by the use of a small harmonica concealed in his mouth. The up and down movement of the accordion could easily have been produced by catching the bottom of the accordion in a loop of black thread, or on a hook. As Carpenter points out, why was the cage *under* the table, instead of above it?[14] There can be no reason other than concealment. A wire cover could have been made for the cage, with an opening for Home's hand.

Crookes responded to W. B. Carpenter's criticism in an article of his own in which he disputes almost all of Carpenter's conclusions.[15] Crookes denies that the phenomena *he* was investigating were anything like the ones that Carpenter had investigated (table turning, raps, and so forth). Crookes refutes the idea that the "actual downward pressure of Mr. Home's fingers" on the board needed to be measured, or was all that important, especially since Home was seated at the time in a "low easy-chair." Crookes reminds Carpenter that he (Crookes) used his entire weight on the board, yet was then only able to get the scale to register slightly more than two pounds. Therefore, Home's actual finger pressure *alone* on the board could not have been responsible for the 6½ pounds that registered on the scale.

Crookes's rebuttal to Carpenter would appear to correctly point out that Carpenter was simply wrong (perhaps maliciously so) about many of the charges he made against Crookes. That does not mean, however, that Crookes's experiments with Home were without fault.

Crookes goes on to quote an article from the *Birmingham Morning News* that takes the position (although not Crookes's true position) that Crookes's research was *anti*spiritualist because he said that the "psychic force" is a result of a direct action *of the medium,* and not of "spirits." It is true that Crookes *did* say this, but his position was not antispiritualist in the loose meaning of the term, because he *did* think that spiritualist mediums were producing genuine effects. He merely realized that he could not *prove* that the effects were due to spirits, nor would the invoking of spirits be the logically correct thing to do (Occam's Razor).

Despite the replies by Crookes to criticisms of his experiments with D. D. Home, there remains one gaping flaw in these experiments. As Podmore points out,[17] this has to do with one of Crookes's stated purposes, namely to establish the occurrence of the new force *under conditions which render fraud impossible.* One way this could have been done was to eliminate the necessity for continuous observation on the part of the experimenter. In the board and scale experiments, this condition was not met.

In a sense, being able to automatically record the weight registered on the scale might have *caused* a different set of problems, namely an increase in the possibility of fraud by Home. It might have made the slipping of a loop of black thread around the far end of the board, underneath the scale, easier. By pulling on *that* end of the board, even at a partially horizontal angle, some greater deflection of the scale could have been achieved than by pressing on the other end of the board. Crookes makes clear in his *Quarterly Journal of Science* articles that what he is recording is a small selection of successful trials extracted from many unsuccessful ones. While the statistical correctness of doing this in most studies is questionable, these may be viewed as "pilot studies" to develop the equipment and protocols. Crookes may therefore be given wider latitude than usual. However, pilot studies are still pilot studies, and cannot be passed off as mature, controlled experiments. As Crookes himself put it,

> the experiments I have tried have been very numerous, but owing to our imperfect knowledge of the conditions which favor or oppose the manifestations of this force, to the apparently capricious manner in which it is exerted, and to the fact that Mr. Home is himself subject to unaccountable ebbs and flows of the force, it has but seldom happened that a result obtained on one occasion could be subsequently confirmed and tested with apparatus specially contrived for the purpose.[18]

In other words, Home was often in a position to dictate the conditions of the experiment. If he didn't like the arrangements, or they were too stringent for him to overcome, all he had to do was to do nothing. No phenomena would occur, and Crookes would have to change the conditions of the experiment. When dealing with a possible conjuror, such an arrangement is unacceptable in "scientific" research.

We must now turn to the case of Herne and Williams, and their relation to William Crookes. This duo of mediums gave a joint séance with D. D. Home for the benefit of Crookes. Florrie Cook also appeared in a joint séance with Herne. The important thing here is that both Herne and Williams were shown conclusively, but separately, to be fakes.[19] Yet both Crookes[20] and Home say that Herne and Williams were genuine. Home claimed, "The well-attested phenomena occurring in the presence of Mr. Williams, whom I have found to be an honest man and one who shrinks from no reasonable tests, all prove the reality of the phenomena."[21] Florence Cook had her joint séance with Herne in 1872.[22] The fact that she had such a sitting has led some to say that they were either both fakes or both authentic. Although that would appear to be the most reasonable conclusion, there is a small possibility that an authentic medium would still choose to appear with a fake. *Why* they would do so is hard to understand.

12

Charges of Fraud Against Home

Although many previous authors have repeated the statement that D. D. Home was never caught in fraud or charged with fraud by anyone, this is simply not the case. Although Home was never *publicly* exposed in a fraud, he was caught (or at least several witnesses *said* he was detected in a fraud) several times. The following are the most notable instances.

The Bare Foot under the Table

An accusation of fraud made against Home that may well *not* be true was that at a séance in 1857 for Napoleon III and his wife, Empress Eugenie, given perhaps at the Tuileries, Home removed his shoe and touched the emperor with his bare foot. The charge was that his socks were cut so that the lower part of the foot was bare. The idea is that Home's bare foot served as a "spirit hand" that touched people. The source of this rumor is difficult to trace. However, I have discovered that it is from Dr. E. Barthez's book, *The Empress Eugenie and Her Circle*. Written as letters during the late 1850s by the physician to the prince (Napoleon III), the book was published in English and French in 1913. In that book, Barthez states quite plainly on pages 164 to 165 that he has discovered how Home did some of his tricks. Mr. Home has, he says, "thin slippers, easily drawn on and off; he has also, I fancy, cuts in his socks, which leave his toes free." This information is based upon the statement of Morio de l'Ile, whom Barthez knew personally.

However, Eugene Osty has shown by the testimony of both Empress Eugenie (in her old age) and Princess Metternich (who was also there) that they believed it to be false.[1] To touch the emperor with a bare foot, even if it was supposed to have been a spirit hand, would have been the height of impertinence. Such an action, had it been discovered, would have been enough to have Home permanently expelled from France. The fact that Home maintained good relations with the empress for several years after this event shows that the incident may not have occurred as reported. Of course, Home may simply have used his foot and been undetected in his actions by the empress or emperor.

On the other hand, there is the article by Count Perovsky-Petrovo-Solovovo, which presents the secondhand testimony of Empress Eugenie from a much earlier period.[2] Eugenie is pictured as saying that she clearly remembered that the incident with Home's bare foot *did* occur. There is also the secondhand testimony of Prince Roland Bonaparte, who said that he was told by the Empress Eugenie that the incident *did* occur. It supposedly happened at Biarritz on 5 September 1857, and not at the Tuileries. The evidence of Professor Cyon of the Imperial Medical Academy in St. Petersburg is also presented, in which he recounts hearing General Fleury's account of the Home séance. Fleury left the sitting, then silently returned to stand behind Home, where he would not be noticed. From this vantage point he saw Home remove his right foot from its shoe and touch *the empress* on the hand with his bare foot. General Fleury then told the séance group what he had seen. Home was escorted to the ferry at Calais the next day by two government agents who had orders to keep the incident secret.

Home's Spirit Hands

There are a number of sittings by D. D. Home, mostly in the early part of his career (1855–65), when "spirit hands" appeared. These usually glowing hands appeared and touched various people seated around the séance table. Among the reasons why the sitters thought these hands were spirit hands and not the hands of Home himself were (1) Home's hands were visible on the top of the table (i.e., they were *not* being held by anyone), and (2) the hands ended at the wrist where nothing further could be seen. It must be remembered that the lights were turned down at this part of the séance.

When Crookes summarized the Home "Hand Phenomena," which he included in his article in the *Quarterly Journal of Science*,[3] he noted that there were a number of different characteristics of the hands. Some were child-sized and some were not. Some were cold and some were warm. Crookes's observations were actually accurate, but, as noted previously, he did not interpret what he saw correctly. He did not examine what conjuring or other basically fraudulent methods could have been used to produce the effects that he saw. Crookes did not suspect a trick, and he accepted the genuineness of what he had observed. Of course, he was then unable to explain what was noted in the terms that he used to describe what he thought he had seen. Some of Crookes's observations, however, do provide us with help in solving the mystery of the spirit hands.

Of prime importance in our investigation is the statement of Mr. F. Merrifield. It was first made anonymously in 1889, and appears as Appendix D in F. W. H. Meyers and W. Barrett's article. In July 1855, Merrifield says,

> We were assembled—about 14 in number—about a round table, occupying the whole circumference of it except a space on the part of it nearest the window, which went down to the floor, or nearly so. Home sat at one end of the horse-shoe formed by the company, in a low easy chair. Bye-and-bye, in the open space between him and the other end of the horse-shoe, a tiny hand—considerably smaller than that of any adult person—could be seen outlined against the faint light of the window, the object rising from the edge of the table, and descending and rising again, and so on several times. It appeared to me that it showed itself mainly at two different points—one about corresponding to the length of Home's arm, the other more distant—about the place of his foot. Some of the company became much excited, and begged, leaning forward, that they might be allowed to "kiss the dear hand." In response to these entreaties the object rose higher and came nearer (still always rising from the edge of the table, the "arm"—apparently in a loose baggy sleeve—rising with it, never suspended in the air), and I thought I could see slight movements in the shoulder or upper part of Home's arm corresponding with the movements, on these occasions, of the "spirit hand." The outline of the upper part of Home's arm seemed, as the "spirit hand" advanced to meet the persons far from the window, and who were leaning towards it, to approach nearer to the "arm," or whatever it was that supported the "spirit hand." The situation at this point struck me so forcibly—the trick so plain to my eyes and the reverential and adoring expressions of the company— among whom I think there were only three, including my wife and myself, who were not firm believers, that I was seized with a strong impulse to laugh. I restrained myself from making any sound, but I felt my shoulders shake: we were wedged closely together, I being next to a lady who must have clearly felt the movement, and clearly did so, for she immediately said she thought they had had enough now; and it was suggested that lights had better be brought in, which was done.[4]

Merrifield later allowed his name to be attached to his statement.

What we have here, thanks to the careful observation of Merrifield, who later said that he saw the entire device attached to Home's arm between the medium's body and the "spirit hand,"[5] is an eyewitness account of fraud on the part of Home.

Robert Browning's Feelings of Fraud

Robert Browning (1812–1889) and his wife, Elizabeth Barrett Browning (1806–1861), differed strongly in their opinion of D. D. Home. Elizabeth liked Home, while Robert hated him. The exact reasons for their feelings about Home remain theoretical, but there has been a good deal of speculation,[6] which has ranged from a fear by Robert that Home was a homosexual, to jealousy by Robert that "the spirits" thought Elizabeth a better poet than he. It should be noted that none of these speculations has been substantiated and, indeed, several have been pretty thoroughly refuted.

Rather than rehash each of these attempts at an explanation, parts of a letter from Robert Browning himself will be quoted, stating what he thought of the Home séance he attended at the Rymer house. Browning wrote Mrs. Elizabeth C. Kinney on 25 July 1855, explaining to her what happened two days previous at the séance. The most relevant parts of this long letter are the following:

> On what I have to observe—first, that I believe in the honesty and veracity of the [Rymer] family—and in their absolute incompetence to investigate a matter of this sort. Next, in the impossibility of a stranger taking the simplest measure for getting at the truth or falsehood of the "manifestations"—it was a family-party, met for family-purposes, and one could no more presume to catch [i.e., grab] at the hands (for instance) of what they believed to be the spirit of their child, than one could have committed any other outrage on their feelings. I heard that somebody who had been there two days before, and had told Mr. H. [Home] "the hand is *yours*"—showed thereby his "forgetting he was in a private house"— so I remembered it, you may be sure. Mr. Wilkie Rymer, the nearest [at the table] to the hand, was more than once desired by Mr. H. [Home] "not to look so closely"—& he refused to touch his brother's hand or drapery "lest it might displease him"—why or wherefore I don't know. I asked if the hands were ever seen away from the table and Mr. Home— they were never so seen, tho' the family speak of spirits passing the windows without [i.e., outside], and other appearances. . . . I shall not much surprise you when I confess that my wife believes in all of the above, *but* the trance, which there was no getting over. She suggests, however, explanations of various kinds, consistent with Mr. H.'s integrity (she thinks it was "not unlike some dissenting sermons she has heard") and I wish

it may be so. On the whole, I think the whole performance most clumsy, and unworthy anybody really setting up for a "medium." I,—the poorest of mechanicians,—can fancy such an obvious contrivance as a tube, fixed or flexible, under Mr. H.'s loose clothes & sack-like *paletot* & inordinate sleeves, which should convey some half dozen strings & no more, to his breast,—for instance,—and work the three fantoccini-hands, after these various fashions—just as he did, and easily. There are probably fifty more ingenious methods at the service of every "prestidigitateur"—I would also operate with lights on the table *always*—challenge people to find out my tricks (as all good jugglers [conjurors] do) and leave the "trance" out altogether.[7]

The Phosphorylated Oil Vial

There is a report that Home was observed looking at a small vial.[8] When Home noticed that he had been observed, he surreptitiously abandoned the vial on the mantelpiece of the room in which he was located. The observer cleverly managed to pick up the vial, slip it in his pocket, and later have its contents analyzed. The contents turned out to be what was then called "oil of phosphorus." This is olive oil in which a lump of white phosphorous has been allowed to dissolve while in an air-tight container. It takes several weeks to do so, but eventually a substance is formed that allows the phosphorous to be finely dispersed in the oil, yet not catch fire when exposed to the air, as a lump of white phosphorous would do. Instead, the phosphorous particles individually oxidize when air is allowed to enter the closed container. The phosphorous gives off light, often enough to allow the container to be used as a flashlight of a sort. It will be recalled that William Crookes used such a light to observe Florence Cook lying upon the chair in the cabinet when Katie King had supposedly been materialized. Unless the container is quite large, the amount of light produced by oil of phosphorous is really very small, not nearly as much as a modern flashlight of the same size would produce.

The question with regard to Home now becomes "What was Home doing with a vial of oil of phosphorous?" There would appear to be no explanation for *both* his possessing it *and* his quickly abandoning it when he noted he was observed, other than the fact that he was planning to use it to produce some effects in a séance. We know that at about this time Home was producing small, glowing "patches," and occasionally glowing hands, in his sittings.[9] The glowing objects were dropped from his séances at some point shortly after this, and never reappear.

The "Lizzie"/"Eliza" Fraud

This is a relatively minor matter, but it tends to show that when Home tried to present individual spirits *by name* (which he rarely did, often claiming that individual personalities could not be contacted as such),[10] he failed. Eliza Lynn Linton, Victorian novelist and women's rights advocate, once attended one of Home's séances. There Home allegedly made contact with "baby Eliza," who had died in 1857 while in Linton's care. However, the baby had *always* been referred to as "Lizzie," never "Eliza," even though it had been named for Eliza Lynn Linton. Linton later fictionalized her account of this incident in her autobiographical novel, *The Autobiography of Christopher Kirkland,* where the baby is called "Christie" instead of "Chrishna," and the medium is called "Mr. Hume."[11]

The Sculpted-Hands Fraud Charge

As has been previously mentioned, Thomas Woolner, a sculptor, has been quoted by Frederick Greenwood as having said that he (Woolner) visited Home's studio in Rome in the year that Home lived there (1863–64) and saw that the studio was filled with sculpted hands. Although merely sculpting hands is *not* a fraudulent action per se, the use of such hands in a séance (as described) would be.[12]

13

Observation and Malobservation

There remains a problem of a different sort from those we have considered in relation to the explanation of D. D. Home's phenomena, namely the problem of malobservation. The fact that a perfectly honest person with good vision can observe a phenomenon and report it incorrectly is well known. Perhaps the most common experimental example of this is the famous classroom robbery experiment, in which a "robber" bursts into a classroom, steals something, and departs.[1] The various members of the class are then asked to describe the "robber" (sometimes he/she is a "murderer"). The descriptions usually vary greatly and are quite contradictory. How does any of this apply to the case of Daniel Dunglas Home and his phenomena?

D. D. Home's séances were occasionally recorded by different people. It will be interesting to compare two such descriptions of the same sitting. In the case of a séance held in October 1855 at the home of Mr. John S. Rymer, both Rymer and Thomas Dalling Barlee published a written version of the sitting. Both descriptions are given side by side in Frank Podmore's *Mediums of the Nineteenth Century*.[2] We can compare the two versions and see that there are many discrepancies, among them a difference about who suggested that a piece of paper and a pencil be placed *under* a tablecloth to receive a message. Rymer says *he* suggested it, Barlee says it was Home who did. Of course, if Home suggested it, it could mean that Home had planned a method for making a message appear, as it did.

Podmore feels that the light conditions during Home's séances were so poor and the mental state of the sitters so receptive or credulous that the presence of Home's hands on the table was not certain. Many of the effects could have been produced, Podmore feels, by the use of Home's feet.[3]

The experiments of S. Davey and Richard Hodgson[4] are important to an understanding of how people can malobserve things in a séance setting. Davey was an accomplished amateur magician with an interest in spiritualism. He was especially good with slates. In those days (circa 1890), there were a number of slate mediums working, the most notable of whom were William Eglinton and Henry Slade. At a slate medium's séance, blank slates (small blackboards) were sealed and when later opened were found to contain the written answers to questions asked by the sitters to "the spirits."

Hodgson and Davey invited a number of carefully chosen witnesses to participate in a séance, including several members of the Society for Psychical Research. Immediately after each séance, the participants were asked to write down exactly what they thought had taken place. Of course, the entire sitting consisted of "tricks" done by Davey and a confederate. Davey also wrote down just what he had done. A comparison of the participants' observations with Davey's notes revealed that even an experienced séance attender is often a poor observer. Edmunds has made a good summary of part of what was observed and of what *actually* occurred:

A Mrs. Johnson stated that before the séance commenced the room was thoroughly searched and the "medium" emptied his pockets. The door was then locked and sealed, the light extinguished, and the sitters, including Davey, held hands around the table. Knocks were heard and bright lights seen, and a musical box which had been placed on the table floated, playing, into the air. The head of a woman appeared, followed by the figure of a man which, after bowing, disappeared through the ceiling. Mrs. Johnson could offer no explanation of the phenomena.

A Miss Wilson also described how the room had been searched and the door secured, and declared that a female head had materialized in good light, after which there appeared a bearded man, who was reading a book and who disappeared through the ceiling. She was certain that Davey's hands were held tightly throughout the séance by the sitters on either side of him, and that when the light was put on afterwards the door was still secured as before the séance commenced.

A third sitter, Mr. Rait, gave an even more dramatic account. He too described the securing of the door, but insisted that nothing was prepared in advance, the sitting being quite a casual one. He claimed to have heard raps and to have been touched by a cold, clammy hand; to have seen a light floating over the sitters which developed into an apparition "frightful in its ugliness," with distinct features resembling the head of a mummy. This was followed by another light which gradually took on the appearance of a bearded Oriental, with stony, fixed eyes and a vacant listless expression. Like the others, he also certified that at the end of the séance the door was still properly locked and sealed.

In actual fact the sitting was quite different from any of these descriptions. Far from being a casual business, the procedure had been thoroughly worked out and rehearsed. Davey *did* lock the door at the beginning of the séance, but immediately unlocked it again. The articles used in the production of the "materializations" were hidden under a bookcase, and were not noticed when the room was searched because Davey created a diversion by turning out his pockets as the searchers approached. The phenomena were engineered by an assistant, a Mr. Munro, who entered by the unlocked door, any noise he made in so doing being drowned by the sound of the musical box. The first "materialization" was a mask covered with muslin (treated with luminous paint), and the second was Mr. Munro standing on the back of the "medium's" chair, his face visible in the reflected light from the pages (also coated with luminous paint) of an open book which he held before him. The noise as the first "spirit" vanished was accidental, but was accepted by the sitters as having been made when the phantom "disappeared through the ceiling." The raps were produced by Munro with a long stick which he had brought with him, and it was he who waved the musical box in the air. The "cold, clammy hand" was also Munro's. He had rolled up his sleeve and held his hand and forearm in a jug of water before entering the room.[5]

Besterman performed a similar study of the weakness of eyewitness accounts of séance sitters' observations. His conclusions were that

(1) There is a slight tendency to underrate the number of persons present at a sitting. (2) Sitters largely ignore disturbances that appear to be irrelevant to the sitting. (3) Sitters are to a considerable extent unable to report with which hand a movement has been performed. (4) The degree to which sitters correctly report the objects used in a sitting is primarily governed, apart from special circumstances, by the size of these objects. (5) Sitters are able only to a very limited extent to report under what conditions of visibility a phenomenon took place. (6) Sitters' reports of auditory conditions at the time of a phenomenon are untrustworthy and erratic. (7) There is a tendency greatly to underrate and greatly to exaggerate a short period of time. (8) Sitters are almost entirely unable to report correctly the scene revealed by a flash [camera]. And (9) Of the illusions that occur the most extreme are those of movement.[6]

While Besterman's conclusions may seem rather commonsensical, they only add another caution to the too ready acceptance of eyewitness testimony.

G. H. Lewes tells of two cases where what was reported to have been observed was quite correct, but the explanation given at first was quite incorrect.[7] He mentions that hundreds of people saw "a large boat with globular silken sails." Four people boarded the boat in a public garden in England (date not specified). At a given signal, the boat with passengers rose from the ground and sailed over the housetops and through the air to France. The explanation was that the sails were actually inflatable balloon-like structures, and the boat was, in fact, a hot-air balloon. Had not this last piece of information been supplied, the reports of what had been observed by all those people, although correct, would have appeared to have violated all known laws of nature and all of past experience.

The other example given by Lewes is something that he witnessed himself (date not specified). A gentleman produced a little cardboard skeleton, which he said would dance on the ground as long as the gentleman kept whistling. He stood the skeleton up on the floor in the center of the room and began whistling. The unsupported skeleton danced with great energy. Several people passed their hands over the skeleton to check for threads; none was found. No use of magnets could be detected. In short, Lewes and his friends were completely mystified, yet they knew there was some sort of conjuring involved. If they had not so known, they may well have concluded that they had seen either spirits or the supernatural at work.

Lewes concludes that great progress with regard to understanding spiritualism will be achieved if and when people start withdrawing their skepticism from the *facts* presented (i.e., admit that there *were* raps and that the furniture moved), and instead concentrate upon the *inferences* (i.e., explanations) that have been given as to the causes of the factual phenomena. This is sound advice.

When a conjuror is at work (as is often the case with mediums), all observations made by sitters need to be taken with an additional large grain of salt. Add to this the fact that most séances occur in dim light and among people who are already conditioned to expect positive spirit phenomena. At least three red warning flags should be up by now because of these three things.

Yet, after Home's sitters supposedly saw some inexplicable phenomenon, the burden of disproof is now placed upon the shoulders of the scientist or skeptic to show that the phenomenon was *not* caused by spirits. This is not to say that *all* phenomena of mediums are simply tricks or malobservation. Each phenomenon must be individually examined and evaluated. However, there certainly were some things produced by D. D. Home, and not so far discussed, that were similar to the levitation witnessed only by feeling Home's boots, while allowing imagination to visualize Home as being above his boots. The use of confederates by Home, although certainly not frequent, may also have played a small role in the production of some of his otherwise inexplicable phenomena.

A fine example of how observation can affect the reporting of a séance phenomenon is reported in Medhurst's article in the series on physical mediums contemporary with Stainton Moses.[8] The article is about some of Home's séances, in this case one in which Ellen Crookes, William's wife, screamed as an apparition approached her. William Crookes's version of this sitting is found in his "Notes of an Enquiry into the Phenomena Called Spiritual," in which he records the following as occurring during a séance with D. D. Home:

> A phantom form came from a corner of the room, took an accordion in its hand, and then glided about the room playing the instrument. The form was visible to all present for many minutes, Mr. Home also being seen at the same time. Coming rather close to a lady who was sitting apart from the rest of the company [i.e., Mrs. Crookes], she gave a slight cry, upon which it vanished.[9]

Twenty years later, Mrs. Crookes was asked about this incident. She then reported that after she had screamed, the figure sank into the floor, still playing the accordion, while it was only one foot above the floor. While one can attribute this additional information to the passage of time having blurred her memory, it is difficult to explain why Stainton Moses's account, written within one day of this same séance which he also attended, makes no mention of the apparition holding or playing an accordion. Surely the accordion playing was one of the most important features of the apparition.

Recent psychological research on the reliability of eyewitness testimony has only tended to bolster the idea that the human brain is a strictly limited mechanism for recording what "really" happened. Studies have shown that postevent suggestions definitely alter what people report has happened.[10] Misled subjects *do* believe they saw the misleading events. There can be a true belief in a false memory. When a conjuror is trying to implant such a false belief, he or she may well succeed. As Woocher reports, because the human mind can process only a small part of what information it receives at any one time, even if we concentrate entirely on visual information, it learns to make conclusions from limited amounts of sensory information.[11] This is done by taking the limited sensory information and integrating it with the fund of general knowledge that has been acquired over a lifetime. In short, Woocher says, witnesses tend to see what they *want* to see. There is a tendency among witnesses to reduce uncertainty by filling in gaps in memory by adding details that were not originally observed, and by changing what they remember so that it "all makes sense." Although this is a strong indictment of the believability of eyewitness testimony, it should be used not to dismiss all such testimony, but rather to require that the more extraordinary the claim made on the basis of that testimony, the more strong the evidence required to back up that claim. The application of all this to the case of D. D. Home should be obvious.

Magicians (conjurors) are quick to utilize the fact that if you don't want someone to see something, you must distract that person's attention away from the event you don't want him to see, and *toward* some other event or object. We can recall the already-mentioned case of Davey turning out his pockets as observers approached the bookcase he didn't want searched.

Part Four

Conclusions

We have begun with an examination of the three major figures in the scientific examination of spiritualism, namely William Crookes, Daniel Dunglas Home, and Florence Cook. We have come to see each of them discredited in some major way. Home was discredited by having been caught in fraud at least five times, and contrary to all previously published sources. Also, all his phenomena have been shown to be produceable without the presence of spirits. As previously known, Florence Cook has been shown to have been caught in fraud *publicly* three times. In addition, her materializations have now been shown to have logical and methodological problems, contradictions in some cases, which render their genuineness highly suspect. For the first time anywhere, Crookes has been discredited for deception, as the logically necessary conclusion from the evidence that he consciously planned and executed the rigging of the Varley test given to Annie Eva Fay to deceive his fellow scientists.

Although it is quite probable that Florrie Cook was fraudulent in her materializations, the role of Crookes in them remains unclear. Florrie Cook has been described as quite short (5′ 2″ tall).[1] The exact quote is "She is a tiny little woman. . . ." We also know that her sister Kate was small and not as pretty as Florence.[2] Several reports make Florence's materialization, Katie King, several inches *taller* than Florrie. All of this points to the use of a confederate on at least some occasions as the only possible solution that would explain the height difference. Yet the two or three times that Florrie's materialization was seized, it proved to be Florrie herself.

What are we to make of this? It would appear that either a confederate was used only on occasion, or else Florrie had discovered a way to make her height appear greater. In the case of the use of a confederate, Crookes

113

must have been aware of it. In the case of Florrie impersonating the materialized Katie King, Crookes, as one who was often inside the medium's cabinet, *must* have been aware that the form in the chair was only a bundle of clothes. No other conclusion seems likely. This would, of course, imply that Crookes was a party to the fraud.

As Trevor Hall has said,

> Few informed students of the case will differ from me in thinking that there are three alternative possibilities in regard to the mediumship of Florence Cook and Crookes's involvement with it. The first is that the phenomena, as reported by Crookes, were genuine. The second is that they were fraudulent, but that Crookes, completely deceived by the medium, mistakenly believed them to be genuine. The third is that they were fraudulent, that Crookes knew they were, and not only reported upon them dishonestly but assisted in the deception. . . . My view is that he could not conceivably have been the dupe of a fraudulent Florence Cook.[3]

If Crookes was, as is suggested, both guilty of conscious deception of his fellow scientists and others in the Varley test of Annie Eva Fay, *and* probably guilty of condoning fraud in the case of Florrie Cook, what are we to make of Crookes's motivation in doing this? Was the motivation entirely sexual in that, as Trevor Hall has suggested in *The Medium and the Scientist,* Crookes was having an affair with Florrie Cook and was using his investigations as a "cover" for the affair? It would appear that Hall's hypothesis is possible, although unlikely. Its probability depends in part upon whether one considers that a so-called "moral lapse" in one area makes it more likely that one would also have a moral lapse in another. We see that Crookes was flawed in his later (1873 and onward) tests of spiritualist mediums. Does that make it likely that he might also cheat on his wife with one of the mediums he was investigating? While he *may* have had an affair with Florrie Cook, it is certain that he did not have one with Annie Eva Fay, and of course not with D. D. Home. So, contrary to what Hall has proposed, the fraud *preceded* the possible affair. The dates involved that establish the probability of the fraud coming first are discussed below. That would also mean that the affair was *not the cause* of the fraud, as Hall has implied. Even if Crookes and Cook *were* having an affair, he seems to have covered up and participated in her fraud for reasons *other* than a desire to prolong or indulge in the affair.

It seems most likely that Crookes's motivation in investigating both Annie Eva Fay and Florrie Cook was the same as it was in Crookes's earlier investigation of D. D. Home, namely a desire to test and hopefully confirm the truth of human survival of death. When Crookes found what he thought was evidence of a new force (having nothing to do with survival of death) as a result of his tests of D. D. Home, he was encouraged that Home's other "powers" (which *did* involve spirits and the survival of death) might also be true. Although Crookes never tested *those* powers *in the laboratory,* he *did* sit and observe many of those supposed powers in the *séance room.* As has been noted, the séance room is a very poor atmosphere in which to conduct research because of its poor lighting, lack of controls, and so forth. It would appear that Home could well have fooled Crookes, both in the laboratory and in the séance room, but there is no evidence that Crookes was a party to any fraud involving D. D. Home.

Yet, as a result of his study of Home, Crookes was "primed" to feel that there was something to spiritualism. When he tried to publish his results in a standard scientific journal of the day, his papers were refused. As a result, he published in the *Quarterly Journal of Science,* which he himself edited. Once those articles began appearing, Crookes had his reputation on the line. He was a proud, vain, and stubborn man, one who was not likely to admit publicly that he had been fooled, even if he were convinced that he had been. When he received negative comments from his scientific peers, it is likely, knowing his personality, that he became more convinced than ever that he would be proved right and eventually vindicated.

As Fournier d'Albe says,

> Crookes also replies to the charge [made by W. B. Carpenter in the *Quarterly Review*] that he commenced the investigation [of D. D. Home] as a convinced spiritualist. "Now let me ask," he exclaims, "what authority has the reviewer for designating me a recent convert to spiritualism? Nothing I have ever written can justify such an unfounded assumption."
>
> This passage, we may say in passing, is open to misinterpretation. At the time it was written [1871] Crookes *was* a spiritualist at heart, and was known to be such by a number of his friends, but he had not published the fact, and evidently did not intend to do so until spiritualism was officially recognised by the scientific authorities in power. He had hopes of himself bringing about the recognition, but knew that he must proceed gradually and carefully.[4]

When Crookes first became aware that Florence Cook was cheating is not known, but let us assume it was before 1 March 1874, when Crookes gave the Varley test to Florence Cook. Although it is implied that she passed, there never was a complete write-up of the test. It is my notion that Crookes gave Florence Cook a resistor of a rating that matched her body resistance, so that she could slip it into the circuit in this case as well as in the test of Mrs. Fay. That would mark the earliest period where we can confidently say that Crookes was involved in fraud with Florrie Cook. Florrie's full-form materializations appear to have started in April 1872, although Crookes does not seem to have investigated Florrie in any formal way until after December 1873. Crookes does seem to have been invited to attend Florrie's séances as early as May 1872. Whether he actually attended is not clear. At any rate, between December 1873 and 1 March 1874 Crookes seems to have become involved to some extent in covering up Florrie Cook's frauds.

With all three of our principals shown to have feet of clay, what does this say about the *scientific* validity of spiritualism? As stated in the Introduction to this book, the question is critically tied to the present examination of it by Crookes, as this is the *only* scientific study of spiritualism that concluded that such phenomena were valid. If Crookes's studies can be shown to be flawed or invalid, the *only* scientific support for spiritualistic phenomena (*and* for D. D. Home as a medium with a previously untarnished reputation) vanishes. That support, it seems to me, has now disappeared as a result of the revelations of the present examination. Spiritualism is left as a much hoped for, but unverified, *religious* outlook.

Notes

Introduction

1. Frank Podmore, *The Newer Spiritualism* (London: T. F. Unwin, 1910), p. 33.

2. Janet Oppenheim, *The Other World: Spiritualism and Psychical Research in England, 1850–1914* (Cambridge, England: Cambridge University Press, 1985), p. 152.

3. Trevor H. Hall, *The Medium and the Scientist: The Story of Florence Cook and William Crookes* (Buffalo, N.Y.: Prometheus Books, 1984). Originally published as *The Spiritualists* (London: G. Duckworth, 1962).

4. D. D. Home, *Incidents In My Life* [First Series] (New York: G. Carleton, 1863; Reprinted by University Books in 1972).

5. Lynn Picknett, *Flights of Fancy?* (London: Ward Lock, 1987).

6. Elizabeth Jenkins, *The Shadow and the Light: A Defence of Daniel Dunglas Home the Medium* (London: Hamish Hamilton, 1982).

7. Horace Wyndham, *Mr. Sludge the Medium: Being the Life and Adventures of Daniel Dunglas Home* (London: G. Bles, 1937).

8. Jean Burton, *Heyday of a Wizard: Daniel Home, the Medium* (New York: Alfred A. Knopf, 1944; London: G. G. Harrap, 1948).

9. William S. Sadler, *The Truth About Spiritualism* (Chicago: A. C. McClurg, 1923), pp. 84–86.

Chapter 1: Biographical Sketch of Florence Cook

1. Trevor H. Hall, *The Medium and the Scientist* (Buffalo, N.Y.: Prometheus Books, 1984), pp. 1–3.

2. R. George Medhurst and K. Mollie Goldney, "William Crookes and the Physical Phenomena of Mediumship," *Proceedings of the Society for Psychical Research* 54, Part 195 (March 1964): 48–49.

3. *The Spiritualist* (January 1872): 9.

4. Most of these biographical details are taken from Trevor H. Hall's research in *The Medium and the Scientist*.

Chapter 2: The Phenomena of Florence Cook

1. *The Spiritualist* (5 June 1872): 47.

2. *The Spiritualist* (31 December 1875): 323.

3. Henry S. Olcott, *People From the Other World* (Hartford, Conn.: American Publishing Co., 1875), pp. 425–78.

4. R. George Medhurst and K. Mollie Goldney, "William Crookes and the Physical Phenomena of Mediumship," *Proceedings of the Society for Psychical Research* 54, Part 195 (March 1964): 57.

5. Trevor H. Hall, *The Medium and the Scientist* (Buffalo, N.Y.: Prometheus Books, 1984), p. 31.

6. Ibid, p. 35.

7. Medhurst and Goldney, p. 57. The original letter is in the Society for Psychical Research D. D. Home Collection as #292.

8. Ibid, p. 60.

9. Ibid, p. 63.

10. E. E. Fournier d'Albe, *The Life of William Crookes* (London: T. Fisher Unwin, 1923; New York: D. Appleton & Co., 1924), pp. 180–81.

11. Quoted from a Crookes letter published in *The Spiritualist* (10 April 1874): 176.

12. *The Spiritualist* (15 May 1874): 230 quotes from the letter of Serjeant Cox.

Chapter 3: Florence's Joint Séances

1. R. George Medhurst and K. Mollie Goldney, "William Crookes and the Physical Phenomena of Mediumship," *Proceedings of the Society for Psychical Research* 54, Part 195 (March 1964): 106–107.

2. Ibid, p. 107.

3. Ibid., pp. 113–14. The original of this most interesting letter is in the Society for Psychical Research Collection currently housed at Cambridge University Library (Home Papers #128B).

4. Also reproduced in Medhurst and Goldney, p. 114.

5. Eric J. Dingwall, *The Critics' Dilemma* (Battle, Sussex [England]: Author, 1966), p. 44.

6. Trevor H. Hall, *The Medium and the Scientist* (Buffalo, N.Y.: Prometheus Books, 1984), pp. 80–81.

7. D. D. Home, *Lights and Shadows of Spiritualism* (London: Virtue, 1877), pp. 326–29. In the Carleton edition (New York, 1877), this is found on pp. 387–90.

8. Dingwall, p. 58.

9. Ibid., p. 59.

10. Ibid., p. 50.

11. *The Spiritualist* (15 May 1874): 230.

12. Dingwall, p. 57.

13. Ibid., p. 68.

14. Ibid., p. 63.

15. Ibid., p. 17.

Chapter 4: Florence Cook's Frauds

1. "Recent Experiences in Spiritualism," *The Lancet* (10 January 1874): 63.

2. *The Spiritualist* (16 June 1874): 34.

3. Osbert Sitwell, *Left Hand, Right Hand* (Boston: Little Brown & Co., 1944). The original version of the exposure is found in the *Evening Standard* newspaper for Monday, 12 January 1880.

4. *The Spiritualist* (1 November 1878): 205; also mentioned in Trevor H. Hall, *The Medium and the Scientist* (Buffalo, N.Y.: Prometheus Books), p. 20n.

5. *Psychische Studien* 26 (1899): 546–51, 604–609; mentioned also in Hall, pp. 158–59.

6. *The Spiritualist* (16 February 1873): 105; also mentioned in Hall, pp. 22–23.

7. "Spirit Forms," *The Spiritualist* (30 March 1874); *The Spiritualist* (5 June 1874): 270–71; also mentioned in Hall, pp. 67–68.

8. Hall, p. 117.

9. Ibid, p. 72.

10. Ibid, pp. 71–72.

11. Ibid, p. 72.

12. Ibid., p. 65.

13. Mercy Phillimore, "L.S.A. Records and Comments," *Light* (3 September 1942): 286.

14. These are modified from John Beloff, "George Zorab and Katie King," in F. W. J. J. Snell, ed., *In Honor of G. A. M. Zorab* (The Hague: Nederlandse Vereniging voor Parapsychologie, 1986), pp. 17–18.

Chapter 5: Biographical Sketch of Sir William Crookes

1. The best biographical sources about Crookes are E. E. Fournier d'Albe, *The Life of Sir William Crookes* (London: T. Fisher Unwin, 1923; New York: D. Appleton & Co., 1924) and the article by W. H. Brock in *The Dictionary of Scientific Biography,* vol. 3 (New York: Charles Scribner's Sons, 1981), pp. 474–82.

2. See John Emsley, "The Trouble with Thallium," *New Scientist* (10 August 1978): 392–94 for details of Claude-Auguste Lamy's claim to have discovered thallium.

Chapter 6: Crookes's Explanations of Spiritualism

1. Also reported in William Crookes, *Crookes and the Spirit World* (London: Souvenir Press, 1972; New York: Taplinger Publishing Co., 1972), pp. 126–29.

2. Ibid., p. 127.

3. Ibid., p. 129.

Chapter 7: Crookes's Motivation

1. E. E. Fournier d'Albe, *The Life of Sir William Crookes* (London: T. Fisher Unwin, 1923; New York: D. Appleton & Co., 1924), pp. 174–75.

2. Ibid., p. 177.

3. Ibid., pp. 175–76.

4. Ibid., pp. 178–79.

5. Trevor H. Hall, *The Medium and the Scientist* (Buffalo, N.Y.: Prometheus Books, 1984), p. 34.

6. John Palfreman, "William Crookes: Spiritualism and Science," *Ethics in Science and Medicine* 3 (1976): 218.

7. W. Barrett, *Proceedings of the Society for Psychical Research* 31 (1921): 20.

8. Reproduced in William Crookes, *Crookes and the Spirit World* (London: Souvenir Press, 1972; New York: Taplinger Publishing Co., 1972), pp. 237–38.

9. Ibid., pp. 238–39.

10. Ibid., p. 230.

11. Ibid., pp. 122–23.

12. Reported in *The Spiritualist* (13 April 1874) and in Crookes, p. 135.

13. *The Spiritualist* (5 June 1874) and Crookes, p. 137.

14. Crookes, p. 138.

15. Eric J. Dingwall, *The Critics' Dilemma* (Battle, Sussex [England]: Author, 1966), pp. 10–11.

16. *The Spiritualist* (26 March 1875): 151.

17. "Cromwell Varley's Electrical Tests," *Journal of the Society for Psychical Research* 43 (1965): 26–31.

18. Hall, p. 47.

19. Ibid., p. 111.

20. R. George Medhurst and K. Mollie Goldney, "William Crookes and the Physical Phenomena of Mediumship," *Proceedings of the Society for Psychical Research* 54, Part 195 (March 1964): 103.

21. *The Spiritualist* (12 March 1875): 126–28; also in Medhurst and Goldney, pp. 95–100.

22. The letter is reproduced in Medhurst and Goldney, pp. 103–104. It originally appeared in *The Spiritualist* (21 December 1877): 293.

23. Dingwall, p. 9.

24. Ian Stevenson, "Reflections on Mr. Trevor Hall's *The Spiritualists,*" *Journal of the Society for Psychical Research* 57 (October 1963): 219.

25. Dingwall, p. 60.

Chapter 8: Biographical Sketch of D. D. Home

1. Among them Jean Burton, *Heyday of a Wizard: Daniel Home, the Medium* (New York: A. A. Knopf, 1944; London: G. G. Harrap, 1948); Horace Wyndham, *Mr. Sludge, the Medium: Being the Life and Adventures of Daniel Dunglas Home, 1833–1886* (London: G. Bles, 1937); I. G. Edmunds, *D. D. Home: The Man Who Talked with Ghosts* (Nashville, Tenn.: Thomas Nelson, 1978); Elizabeth Jenkins, *The Shadow and the Light: A Defence of D. D. Home the Medium* (London: Hamish Hamilton, 1982); and the two hagiographies by Mrs. Home, *The Gift of D. D. Home* (London: Kegan Paul Trench, Trubner, 1890) and *D. D. Home: His Life and Mission* (London: Trubner, 1888; also reprint, New York: Arno Press, 1976).

2. Trevor H. Hall, *The Enigma of Daniel Home: Medium or Fraud?* (Buffalo, N.Y.: Prometheus Books, 1984).

3. Ibid., pp. 18–19.

4. Ibid., p. 29.

5. The best summary of what went on between Jane Lyon and Home is found in H. Arthur Smith's summary in *Journal of the Society for Psychical Research* 4 (July 1889): 117–19.

6. As Paul Tabori states in the chapter "D. D. Home: The Medium of Kings" in his *Companions of the Unseen* (New Hyde Park, N.Y.: University Books, 1968), p. 76.

7. Suggested by Eric J. Dingwall in his "D. D. Home: Sorcerer of Kings" in his *Some Human Oddities* (London: Howe and Vin Thal, 1947; New Hyde Park, N.Y.: University Books, 1962), p. 126.

8. Reported in 6 Law Reports Equity Cases 655.

9. Hall, pp. 53–68.

10. Ibid., pp. 69–81.

11. D. D. Home, *Lights and Shadows of Spiritualism* (New York: G. W. Carleton, 1877; London: Virtue, 1877), pp. 280–320.

12. Ibid., p. 415.

13. Ibid., p. 416.

14. F. W. H. Meyers and W. Barrett, "D. D. Home, His Life and Mission," *Journal of the Society for Psychical Research* 4 (July 1889): 101.

15. Ibid., p. 104.

16. Home Papers, Cambridge University Library, #705.

Chapter 9: Home's Phenomena

1. H. D. Jencken, "New Spirit Manifestations," *Spiritual Magazine* (January 1868): 30–36; also quoted in Herbert Thurston, "Bodily Elongation," *The Month* (December 1936): 539–40.

2. H. D. Jencken, "Elongation of Mr. Home, with Measurements," *Human Nature* 3 (1869): 138–41.

3. See Milbourne Christopher, *ESP, Seers and Psychics* (New York: Thomas Y. Crowell, 1970), pp. 183–84.

4. Ricky Jay, *Learned Pigs & Fireproof Women* (New York: Villard Books, 1986), pp. 38–42.

5. *Report on Spiritualism of the Committee of the London Dialectical Society,* pp. 207, 213–14; also quoted in Frank Podmore, *Mediums of the 19th Century,* vol. 2 (New Hyde Park, N.Y.: University Books, 1963), p. 259.

6. *Report on Spiritualism of the Committee of the London Dialectical Society,* pp. 213–14.

7. William Crookes, "Notes of an Enquiry Into the Phenomena Called Spiritual," *Quarterly Journal of Science* (January 1874); also reported in William Crookes, *Researches in the Phenomena of Spiritualism* (London: J. Burns, 1874); William Crookes, *Crookes and the Spirit World* (London: Souvenir Press, 1972; New York: Taplinger Publishing Co., 1972), pp. 118–19.

8. Frederick Greenwood, "The Medium 'Sludge' and the Poet Browning," *The Realm* (11 January 1895). Greenwood quotes Thomas Woolner, a sculptor, who saw the hands in Home's studio in Rome.

9. Merrifield's statement appears as "A Sitting With D. D. Home" in *Journal of the Society for Psychical Research* 11 (May 1903): 76–80.

10. Christopher, p. 183.

11. William Crookes, "Notes of Seances With D. D. Home," *Proceedings of the Society for Psychical Research* 6 (1889): 103–104.

12. Barbara Honywood, "Appendix M," *Journal of the Society for Psychical Research* 4 (July 1889): 135–36.

13. Reported in [W. B. Carpenter's] anonymous "Spiritualism and its Recent Converts," *Quarterly Review* 131 (October 1871): 334–35.

14. See, for example, Joseph Jastrow, *Error and Eccentricity in Human Belief* (New York: Dover Publications, 1962), pp. 140–41. The book was formerly called *Wish and Wisdom, Episodes in the Vagaries of Belief* (1935).

15. See, for example, William Crookes's "Experimental Investigation of a New Force," *Quarterly Journal of Science* (July 1871), reprinted in Crookes, *Crookes and the Spirit World*, pp. 23–27.

16. William Crookes, "Notes of Seances With D. D. Home," *Proceedings of the Society for Psychical Research* 6 (1889): 113; also, *Human Nature* 4 (1870): 86.

17. James Randi, personal communication, 1990.

18. Hamilton Aïde, "Was I Hypnotized?" *Nineteenth Century* 27 (April 1890): 579.

19. William Gresham, "King of the Spook Workers," in Alexander Klein, *The Double Dealers* (Philadelphia: J. B. Lippincott, 1958), pp. 129–43. Originally published in *Argosy* (1957).

20. Eric J. Dingwall, "D. D. Home: Sorcerer of Kings," in his *Some Human Oddities* (London: Howe and Vin Thal, 1947; New Hyde Park, N.Y.: University Books, 1962), p. 94.

21. Discussed in a muddled sort of way in Mrs. Home's *D. D. Home: His Life and Mission* (London: Trubner, 1888; reprint, New York: Arno Press, 1976), pp. 410–415.

22. Mrs. E. M. Ward (Henrietta Mary Ada Ward), *Memories of Ninety Years,* 2d ed. (New York: Henry Holt, 1925), p. 102.

Chapter 10: The D. D. Home Levitations

1. H. D. Jencken, "Mr. Home's Manifestations," *Human Nature* 3 (December 1868): 50.

2. Lord Adare, *Experiences in Spiritualism With Mr. D. D. Home* (Privately published, 1869; reprint, London: The Society for Psychical Research, 1924, and New York: Arno Press, 1976), pp. 82–83.

3. Trevor H. Hall, *The Enigma of Daniel Home: Medium or Fraud?* (Buffalo, N.Y.: Prometheus Books, 1984), pp. 103–138.

4. Frank Podmore, *The Newer Spiritualism* (London: T. Fisher Unwin, 1910), p. 68.

5. Archie Jarman, "How D. D. Home Got His Feat Off the Ground?" *Alpha,* no. 9 (October 1980): 9–12.

6. Alice Johnson, "The Education of the Sitter," *Proceedings of the Society for Psychical Research* 21 (February 1909): 495–96.

7. Podmore, pp. 60–61.

8. "J. G. C.," *Spiritual Magazine* 6 (1890): 89.

9. William Crookes, "Sittings With D. D. Home," *Proceedings of the Society for Psychical Research* 6 (1889): 118–19.

Chapter 11: D. D. Home and William Crookes

1. E. E. Fournier d'Albe, *Life of Sir William Crookes* (London: T. Fisher Unwin, 1923; New York: D. Appleton & Co., 1924), p. 190.

2. K. M. Goldney, "Introduction," in William Crookes, *Crookes and the Spirit World* (New York: Taplinger Publishing Co., 1972), pp. 5–6.

3. William Crookes, "Spiritualism Viewed by the Light of Modern Science," *Quarterly Journal of Science* (July 1870): 318; also Crookes, *Crookes and the Spirit World,* p. 17.

4. William Crookes, "Spiritualism Viewed by the Light of Modern Science," p. 317; also Crookes, *Crookes and the Spirit World,* p. 16.

5. Robert Hare, *Experimental Investigation of the Spirit Manifestations Demonstrating the Existence of Spirits and Their Communion with Mortals* (New York: Partridge and Brittan, 1855), p. 48.

6. William Crookes, "Some Further Experiments on Psychic Force," *Quarterly Journal of Science* (October 1871): 477; also, William Crookes, *Researches in the Phenomena of Spiritualism* (London: J. Burns, 1874), and Crookes, *Crookes and the Spirit World,* p. 41.

7. William Crookes, *Quarterly Journal of Science* (July 1871): 339; also Crookes, *Crookes and the Spirit World,* p. 22.

8. William Crookes, "Notes of Seances With D. D. Home," *Proceedings of the Society for Psychical Research* 6 (1889): 99.

9. The test is described in "Experimental Investigation of a New Force," *Quarterly Journal of Science* (July 1871), and reprinted in Crookes, *Crookes and the Spirit World,* pp. 24, 28–29.

10. Letters from Stokes to Crookes and Crookes's replies, Stokes Papers, Cambridge University Library, C1066, C1068, C1069, C1071, C1073.

11. Hare, p. 51.

12. Crookes, *Crookes and the Spirit World,* pp. 45, 50–54.

13. [W. R. Carpenter], "Spiritualism and Its Present Converts," *Quarterly Review* (October 1871): 345.

14. Ibid., p. 346.

15. William Crookes, "Psychic Force and Modern Spiritualism: A Reply to the *Quarterly Review,*" from *Researches in the Phenomena of Spiritualism,* pp. 45–72; reprinted in Crookes, *Crookes and the Spirit World,* pp. 61–92.

16. Crookes, *Researches in the Phenomena of Spiritualism,* pp. 61–66; reprinted in Crookes, *Crookes and the Spirit World,* pp. 80–86.

17. Frank Podmore, *Mediums of the 19th Century,* vol. 2 (New Hyde Park, N.Y.: University Books, 1963), p. 239.

18. Crookes, *Researches in the Phenomena of Spiritualism,* p. 10; also, Crookes, *Crookes and the Spirit World,* p. 23.

19. Williams was caught cheating in 1878 in Holland, see Trevor H. Hall, *The Medium and the Scientist* (Buffalo, N.Y.: Prometheus Books, 1984), p. 10. Herne was caught producing fake spirit photographs in 1872, see *The Spiritualist* (5 June 1872): 47; also reported in R. George Medhurst and K. Mollie Goldney, "William Crookes and the Physical Phenomena of Mediumship," *Proceedings of the Society for Psychical Research* 54, Part 195 (March 1964): 49–50. He was also caught impersonating John King, see *The Spiritualist* (31 December 1875) and Medhurst and Goldney, p. 50.

20. William Crookes in *The Spiritualist* (19 June 1874); also printed in Medhurst and Goldney, p. 106.

21. Draft in D. D. Home's writing for *Lights and Shadows of Spiritualism* (evidently not used there, but written in 1875–1876) in the D. D. Home papers at Cambridge University; mentioned also in Medhurst and Goldney, p. 46, note 2.

22. See *The Spiritualist* (15 May 1872): 34, and also Hall, *The Medium and the Scientist,* p. 11.

Chapter 12: Charges of Fraud Against Home

1. E. Osty, "D. D. Home: New Light on the Exposure at the Tuileries," *Journal of the American Society for Psychical Research* 30, no. 3 (March 1936): 77–93 and 30, no. 4 (April 1936): 120–26.

2. V. Perovsky-Petrovo-Solovovo, "Some Thoughts on D. D. Home," *Proceedings of the Society for Psychical Research* 39 (March 1930): 247–65.

3. William Crookes, "Notes of an Enquiry Into the Phenomena Called Spiritual," *Quarterly Journal of Science* (January 1874); also reprinted in William Crookes, *Researches in the Phenomena of Spiritualism* (London: J. Burns, 1874) and William Crookes, *Crookes and the Spirit World* (London: Souvenir Press, 1972; New York: Taplinger Publishing Co., 1972), pp. 118–19.

4. F. W. H. Meyers and W. Barrett, "D. D. Home, His Life and Mission," *Journal of the Society for Psychical Research* 4 (July 1889): 121–22.

5. Merrifield's statement appears as "A Sitting With D. D. Home," *Journal of the Society for Psychical Research* 11 (May 1903): 76–80.

6. See, among others, Elizabeth Jenkins, *The Shadow and the Light: A Defence of D. D. Home the Medium* (London: Hamish Hamilton, 1982); William Lyon Phelps, "Robert Browning on Spiritualism," *Yale Review* 23 (1933): 125–38; Trevor H. Hall, *The Enigma of Daniel Home: Medium or Fraud?* (Buffalo, N.Y.: Prometheus Books, 1984); and Eric J. Dingwall, "D. D. Home: Sorcerer of Kings," in *Some Human Oddities* (London: Howe & Vin Thal, 1947; New Hyde Park, N.Y.: University Books, 1962), pp. 91–128.

7. The letter is reproduced in Phelps, "Robert Browning on Spiritualism," pp. 125–38.

8. The charge was related by Robert Browning as an incident that was told to him by a lady who was told it by the man who had observed Home with the oil of phosphorous. This thirdhand account weakens the story considerably. It is reported in the *Journal of the Society for Psychical Research* (July 1889): 102, and repeated in Horace Wyndham, *Mr. Sludge, the Medium: Being the Life and Adventures of Daniel Dunglas Home, 1833–1886* (London: G. Bles, 1937), p. 146.

9. The glowing hands are reported in Crookes, *Crookes and the Spirit World,* p. 218, among other places.

10. See Nancy Fix Anderson, *Woman Against Women in Victorian England: A Life of Eliza Lynn Linton* (Bloomington, Ind.: Indiana University Press, 1987), pp. 142–43.

11. Elizabeth Lynn Linton, *The Autobiography of Christopher Kirkland*, pp. 17–22.

12. Frederick Greenwood, *The Realm* (11 January 1895).

Chapter 13: Observation and Malobservation

1. The most sophisticated version of this is reported by Robert Buckhout, "Eyewitness Testimony," *Scientific American* 231 (December 1974): 29, but the experiments go back to H. Munsterberg, *On the Witness Stand* (New York: Doubleday, 1908), pp. 49–54.

2. Frank Podmore, *Mediums of the 19th Century*, vol. 2 (New Hyde Park, N.Y.: University Books, 1963), pp. 233–36.

3. Ibid., p. 236.

4. Richard Hodgson, "The Possibilities of Malobservation and Lapse of Memory from a Practical Point of View," *Proceedings of the Society for Psychical Research* 4 (1886–1887): 381–405; and Richard Hodgson, "Mr. Davey's Imitations by Conjuring of Phenomena Sometimes Attributed to Spirit Agency," *Proceedings of the Society for Psychical Research* 8 (1892): 253–310.

5. Simeon Edmunds, "Psychological Elements in Spiritualistic Testimony," *International Journal of Parapsychology* 6 (1964): 291–92.

6. Theodore Besterman, "The Psychology of Testimony in Relation to Paraphysical Phenomena: A Report of an Experiment," *Proceedings of the Society for Psychical Research* 40 (1931–1932): 363–87.

7. [G. H. Lewes], "Seeing is Believing," *Blackwood's Edinburgh Magazine* 88 (October 1860): 383–84.

8. R. G. Medhurst, "Stainton Moses and Contemporary Physical Mediums. 10: Daniel Dunglas Home," *Light* 85 (1965): 91–92.

9. William Crookes, *Quarterly Journal of Science* (January 1874); reprinted in William Crookes, *Crookes and the Spirit World* (London: Souvenir Press, 1972; New York: Taplinger Publishing Co., 1972), pp. 121 and 219.

10. See Kelly Toland, Hunter Hoffman, and Elizabeth Loftus, "How Suggestion Plays Tricks with Memory," in John F. Schumaker (ed.), *Human Suggestibility* (New York: Routledge, 1991), pp. 235–52.

11. Fredric D. Woocher, *Stanford Law Review* 29 (1977): 980–83.

Conclusions

1. Mrs. Everett, in the Everett Diaries (in the Society for Psychical Research Collection) says this in a sitting of 14 November 1881. See R. George Medhurst and K. Mollie Goldney, "William Crookes and the Physical Phenomena of Mediumship," *Proceedings of the Society for Psychical Research* 54, Part 195 (March 1964): 72.

2. J. W. Fletcher describes her as "below the average height." Mrs. Everett (see previous note) says Florrie was "much prettier than Miss [Kate] Cook." See Medhurst and Goldney, pp. 72 and 74.

3. Trevor H. Hall, *Florence Cook and William Crookes: A Footnote to an Enquiry* (London: Tomorrow Books, 1963), p. 5.

4. E. E. Fournier d'Albe, *The Life of Sir William Crookes* (London: T. Fisher Unwin, 1923; New York: D. Appleton & Co., 1924), p. 215.

Bibliography

Although every item listed in this bibliography has been read by the author of this book, not all have been cited in the footnotes. The reasons for this are as follows: (1) the footnotes were kept to a bare minimum, (2) many of the items are important in subtle ways, shaping the positions taken, without being specific enough to be footnoted, and (3) it was thought desirable to list for readers many of the difficult-to-identify books and articles on this subject to make it easier for future scholars to locate them. If the amount of work it took for me to track down some of these items is any indication, this will be a worthwhile service in itself. Full bibliographic information has been provided whenever possible.

The manuscript sources used in the preparation of this book include the D. D. Home papers, the R. G. Medhurst/K. M. Goldney papers, and the Crookes papers at the Cambridge University Library (from the Society for Psychical Research collection); the Eric J. Dingwall and Trevor Hall scrapbooks and Dingwall Index files in the Harry Price Collection at the University of London; and the Alfred Russel Wallace papers at the British Library. Typescripts were consulted of the Florence Cook/Charles Blackburn letters, formerly at the Britten Memorial Library in Manchester, but now in storage (and inaccessible) at the Spiritualist National Union center in Stansted. The Harry Houdini scrapbooks at the Library of Congress were also consulted. They contain much ephemeral material on the tricks used by mediums.

Spiritualist Journals

The following spiritualist journals, mostly from the nineteenth century, were extensively examined for articles relating to D. D. Home, Florence Cook, or William Crookes: *Human Nature, Light, Medium & Daybreak, Revue Spirite, Spiritual Magazine,* and *The Spiritualist.*

Books and Articles

Abbott, David P. *Behind the Scenes With the Mediums.* Chicago: Open Court, 1908.

Adare, Lord. *Experiences in Spiritualism with D. D. Home.* N.p., privately published [1869]. Reprint. New York: Arno Press, 1976; and London: Society for Psychical Research, 1924.

Adepte, Un [pseud]. *Katie King: Histoire des ses Apparitions.* Paris: P. G. Leymarie, 1899.

Aïde, Hamilton. "Was I Hypnotised?" *Nineteenth Century* 27 (April 1890): 576–81.

Amberley, [Lord]. "Experiences of Spiritualism." *Fortnightly Review,* n.s., 15 (January 1874): 84–91.

Barnum, P. T. *Humbugs of the World.* New York: Carleton, 1866.

Barrett, William. [Sir William Crookes Testimonial]. *Proceedings of the Society for Psychical Research,* 31 (1921): 12–29.

Barrett, W[illiam] F., and F. W. H. Myers. "D. D. Home, His Life and Mission." *Journal for the Society for Psychical Research* 4 (1889): 101–136.

Barthez, E. [Antoine Charles Ernest Barthez]. *The Empress Eugenie and Her Circle.* New York: Brentano's, 1913.

[Bell, Robert]. "Stranger Than Fiction." *Cornhill Magazine* 2 (August 1860): 211–24.

Besterman, Theodore. "The Psychology of Testimony in Relation to Paraphysical Phenomena: A Report of an Experiment." *Proceedings of the Society for Psychical Research* 40 (1931–1932): 363–87.

Bormann, Walter. *Der Schotte Home: Ein Physiopsychischer Zeuge des Transscendenten im 19. Jahrhundert.* Leipzig [Germany]: Oswald Mutze, 1899.

Brandon, Ruth. *The Spiritualists: The Passion for the Occult in the Nineteenth and Twentieth Centuries.* Buffalo, N.Y.: Prometheus Books, 1984. Reprint of A. A. Knopf, 1983, edition.

Brookes-Smith, Colin. "Cromwell Varley's Electrical Tests." *Journal of the Society for Psychical Research* 43 (1965): 26–31.

Buckhout, Robert. "Eyewitness Testimony." *Scientific American* 231 (December 1974): 23–31, 166.

Burton, Jean. *Heyday of a Wizard: Daniel Home, the Medium.* New York: A. A. Knopf, 1944; London: G. G. Harrap, 1948.

Carpenter, William B. "Mesmerism, Odylism, Table-Turning and Spiritualism." *Fraser's Magazine,* Part 1: n.s., 15 (1877): 136–57; Part 2: n.s., 15 (1877): 382–405.

———. "On the Fallacies of Testimony in Relation to the Supernatural." *Contemporary Review* (January 1876): 279–95.

———. "Psychological Curiousities of Spiritualism." *Fraser's Magazine,* n.s., 16 (1877): 541–63.

———. "Spiritualism and Its Recent Converts." *Quarterly Review* 131 (October 1871): 301–353.

———. "Spiritualism, as Related to Religion and Science." *Fraser's Magazine* 71 (1865): 22–42.

Carrington, Hereward. *The Physical Phenomena of Spiritualism.* New York: American Universities Publishing Co., 1920.

Christopher, Milbourne. "The Medium Who Was Never Exposed." In *ESP, Seers and Psychics,* pp. 174–87. New York: Thomas Y. Crowell, 1970.

Crookes, William. *Crookes and the Spirit World.* London: Souvenir Press, 1972. Also New York: Taplinger Publishing Co., 1972. Edited by R. George Medhurst, with Introduction by K.M. Goldney.

———. "Notes of Séances With D. D. Home." *Proceedings of the Society for Psychical Research* 6 (1889): 98–127.

———. *Researches in the Phenomena of Spiritualism.* London: J. Burns, 1874.

Dingwall, Eric J. *The Critics' Dilemma: Further Comments on Some Nineteenth Century Investigations.* Battle, Sussex, England: Author, 1966.

———. "D. D. Home: Sorcerer of Kings." In *Some Human Oddities,* pp. 91–128. London: Howe & Vin Thal, 1947; New Hyde Park, N.Y.: University Books, [1962].

———. "A Record of Five Sittings With Florence Cook." *Journal of the American Society for Psychical Research* 15 (November 1921): 499–519.

Ducasse, C[urt] J. *A Critical Examination of the Belief in a Life After Death.* Springfield, Ill.: Charles C. Thomas, 1961.

Edmunds, I. G. *D. D. Home: The Man Who Talked with Ghosts.* Nashville, Tenn.: Thomas Nelson, 1978.

Edmunds, Simeon. "Psychological Elements in Spiritualistic Testimony." *International Journal of Parapsychology* 6 (1964): 289–307.

Emsley, John. "The Trouble with Thallium." *New Scientist* (10 August 1978): 392–94.

Evans, Henry Ridgely. *The Spirit World Unmasked.* Chicago: Laird & Lee, n.d. [c 1908].

Fournier d'Albe, E. E. *The Life of Sir William Crookes, O.M., F.R.S..* London: T. Fisher Unwin, 1923; New York: D. Appleton & Co., 1924.

———. *New Light on Immortality.* London: Longmans, Green, 1908.

Gardy, Louis. *Le Medium D. D. Home, Sa Vie et Son Charactere.* Paris: Librairie du Magnetisme, n.d.

Gauld, Alan. *The Founders of Psychical Research.* New York: Schocken Books, 1968.

Gibbons, Frederick X., and Sue Boney McCoy. "Self-Perception and Self-Deception: The Role of Attention in Suggestibility Processes." In *Human Suggestibility,* ed. John F. Schumaker, pp. 185–99. New York: Routledge, 1991.

Gresham, William Lindsay. "King of the Spook Workers." In *The Double Dealers,* ed. Alexander Klein, pp. 129–43. Philadelphia: J. B. Lippincott, 1958.

Hall, Trevor H. *The Enigma of Daniel Home: Medium or Fraud?* Buffalo, N.Y.: Prometheus Books, 1984.

———. *Florence Cook and William Crookes: A Footnote to an Enquiry.* [London]: Tomorrow Books, 1963.

———. *The Medium and the Scientist.* Buffalo, N.Y.: Prometheus Books, 1984. Published in the United Kingdom as *The Spiritualists.* London: Duckworth, 1962.

———. *New Light on Old Ghosts.* London: Gerald Duckworth, n.d.

Hare, Robert. *Experimental Investigation of the Spirit Manifestations, Demonstrating the Existence of Spirits and Their Communion With Mortals.* New York: Partridge & Brittan, 1856.

Hodgson, Richard. "Mr. Davey's Imitations by Conjuring of Phenomena Sometimes Attributed to Spirit Agency." *Proceedings of the Society for Psychical Research* 8 (1892): 253–310.

———. "The Possibilities of Malobservation and Lapse of Memory from a Practical Point of View." *Proceedings of the Society for Psychical Research* 4 (1886–1887): 381–405.

Home, D[aniel] D[unglas]. *Incidents in My Life* [First Series]. New York: G. W. Carleton, 1863; London: Longman, Roberts & Green, 1863.

———. *Incidents in My Life* [Second Series]. New York: Holt & Williams, 1872; London: Tinsley, 1872.

———. *Lights and Shadows of Spiritualism.* New York: G. W. Carleton, 1877; London: Virtue, 1877.

Home, Mrs. D. D. *D. D. Home: His Life and Mission.* London: Trubner, 1888; reprint, New York: Arno Press, 1976.

———. *The Gift of D. D. Home.* London: Kegan Paul, Trench, Trubner, 1890.

Houdini, [Harry]. *A Magician Among the Spirits.* New York: Harper & Brothers, 1924.

Inglis, Brian. *Natural and Supernatural: A History of the Paranormal from Earliest Times to 1914.* Garden City Park, N.Y.: Avery Publishing Group, 1992. Revised edition of 1977 Hodder & Stoughton book.

Jarman, Archie. "How D. D. Home Got His Feat Off the Ground?" *Alpha,* no. 9 (October 1980): 9–12.

Jay, Ricky. *Learned Pigs & Fireproof Women.* New York: Villard Books, 1986.

Jenkins, Elizabeth. *The Shadow and the Light: A Defence of D. D. Home the Medium.* London: Hamish Hamilton, 1982.

Johnson, Alice. "The Education of the Sitter." *Proceedings of the Society for Psychical Research* 21 (1907–1909): 483–511.

Keene, M. Lamar. *The Psychic Mafia.* New York: St. Martin's Press, 1976.

[Lewes, G.H.]. "Seeing Is Believing." *Blackwood's Edinburgh Magazine* 88 (October 1860): 381–95.

London Dialectical Society. *Report on Spiritualism, of the Committee of the London Dialectical Society, Together with the Evidence, Oral and Written, and a Selection from the Correspondence.* London: J. Burns, 1873.

Maskelyne, John Nevil. *Modern Spiritualism: A Short Account of Its Rise and Progress, With Some Exposures of So-Called Spirit Media.* London: Frederick Warne, n.d.

Massey, C. C. "The Possibilities of Malobservation in Relation to Evidence for the Phenomena of Spiritualism." *Proceedings of the Society for Psychical Research* 4 (1886–1887): 75–110.

Medhurst, R. G., and K. M. Goldney. "William Crookes and the Physical Phenomena of Mediumship." *Proceedings of the Society for Psychical Research* 54, Part 195 (March 1964).

Mullholland, John. *Beware Familiar Spirits.* New York: Charles Scribner's Sons, 1938.

Oppenheim, Janet. *The Other World: Spiritualism and Psychical Research in England, 1850–1914.* Cambridge, England: Cambridge University Press, 1985.

Palfreman, John. "William Crookes: Spiritualism and Science." *Ethics in Science and Medicine* 3 (1976): 211–27.

Perovsky-Petrovo-Solovovo, Count. "On the Alleged Exposure of D. D. Home in France." *Journal of the Society for Psychical Research* 15 (1911–1912): 274–88.

Phelps, William Lyon. "Robert Browning on Spiritualism." *Yale Review* 23 (1933): 125–38.

Picknett, Lynn. *Flights of Fancy?: 100 Years of Paranormal Experiences.* London: Ward Lock, 1987.

Podmore, Frank. *Mediums of the 19th Century.* 2 vols. New Hyde Park, N.Y.: University Books, 1963. Reprint of Podmore's *Modern Spiritualism* (1902).

———. *The Newer Spiritualism,* London: T. F. Unwin, 1910.

Price, Harry, and Eric J. Dingwall, eds. *Revelations of a Spirit Medium.* London: Kegan Paul, Trench, Trubner, 1922. Facsimile edition, with notes, of 1891 anonymous edition [thought to be by Charles F. Pidgeon, or someone named Donovan], published by Farrington & Co. of Minneapolis.

Proskauer, Julien J. *Spook Crooks! Exposing the Secrets of the Propheteers Who Conduct Our Wickedest Industry.* New York: A. L. Burt, 1932.

Rinn, Joseph F. *Sixty Years of Psychical Research.* New York: Truth Seeker Co., 1950.

Sadler, William S. *The Truth About Spiritualism.* Chicago: A. C. McClurg, 1923.

Snell, F. W. J. J., ed. *In Honor of G. A. M. Zorab.* [The Hague]: Nederlandse Vereniging voor Parapsychologie, 1986.

Stevenson, Ian. "Reflections on Trevor Hall's *The Spiritualists.*" *Journal of the Society for Psychical Research* 57 (October 1963): 213–26.

Tabori, Paul. "D. D. Home: The Medium of Kings." In *Companions of the Unseen,* pp. 59–80. New Hyde Park, N.Y.: University Books, 1968.

Thurston, Herbert. *The Church and Spiritualism.* Milwaukee: Bruce Publishing, 1933.

Tischner, Rudolf. *Das Medium D. D. Home: Untersuchungen und Beobachtungen.* Leipzig: Oswald Mutze, 1925.

Toland, Kelly, Hunter Hoffman, and Elizabeth Loftus. "How Suggestion Plays Tricks With Memory." In *Human Suggestibility,* ed. John F. Schumaker, pp. 235–52. New York: Routledge, 1991.

Truesdell, John W. *The Bottom Facts Concerning the Science of Spiritualism: Derived from Careful Investigations Covering a Period of Twenty-Five Years.* New York: G. W. Dillingham, 1892.

Walsh, Theobald. *Dunglas Home et le Spiritualisme Americain.* Paris: J. Claye, 1858.

Ward, Mrs. E. M. [Henrietta Mary Ada]. *Memories of Ninety Years,* 2d ed. New York: Henry Holt, 1925.

Watraszewski, X. V. "Uber die Sitzungen mit Mrs. Corner (Florence Cook) zu Warschau im Juni 1899." *Psychische Studien* 26 (October 1899): 546–51, and *Psychische Studien* 26 (November 1899): 604–609.

Woocher, Fredric D. "Did Your Eyes Deceive You? Expert Psychological

Testimony on the Unreliability of Eyewitness Identification." *Stanford Law Review* 29 (1977): 969–1030.

Wyndham, Horace. *Mr. Sludge, the Medium: Being the Life and Adventures of Daniel Dunglas Home, 1833–1886.* London: G. Bles, 1937.

Zorab, George. *D. D. Home, Il Medium.* Milan: Armenia Editore, 1976.

———. *Katie King: Een Geest in Menselijke Gedaante.* Amsterdam: Leopold, 1988.

———. "Were D. D. Home's 'Spirit Hands' Ever Fraudulently Produced?" *Journal of the Society for Psychical Research* 46 (December 1971): 228–35.

Index